Table of Contents

Navigating the VA

Raï

Dedication

I WOULD LIKE TO BEGIN by expressing my heartfelt gratitude to my beloved mother, father, wife, and child for their unwavering support and encouragement throughout the writing of this book. It is your steadfast belief in me and my abilities that has been the driving force behind this project, and I am endlessly grateful for your presence in my life.

I dedicate this book to you as a testament to the depth of my love and appreciation for all that you do. Your kindness, intelligence, and compassion continue to inspire me every day, and I am honored to have you all by my side, both physically and spiritually, as I pursue my passions.

May this book serve as a symbol of the love and gratitude I hold for you and as a reminder of the profound impact you have had on my life. Thank you for being my constant companions, my rocks, and my greatest supporters.

In addition to the collective wisdom and guidance, there are some words from my parents that have particularly stuck with me over the years, shaping my thoughts and actions as I grew and learned.

My father, a man of few but impactful words, once told me, "You'll be lucky if you can find three good people you can consider a friend when you're older. Just never kiss butts." It was a message about the rarity of genuine friendship and the importance of staying true to oneself. His advice was spot on, and I carry it with me to this day. Thank you, Dad, for teaching me the value of authenticity and integrity.

My mother, a woman of faith and humor, often told me, "Stop worrying about it and put it in God's hands." It was her way of teaching me to let go of anxieties and trust in a higher power. She also had a playful piece of advice, "When a girl starts punching you, give her a good shake and walk away." That one always made me laugh. Mom, your words have taught me to face life with a sense of humor and unwavering faith.

You have both transitioned to your rest, yet your words and lessons live on within me. I am truly blessed to be your son, and I have no complaints. Your wisdom continues to guide my path, and I am forever grateful for the legacy you left behind.

With all my heart, Raï-CTA

Acknowledgment

I AM GRATEFUL TO BEGIN by expressing my sincere appreciation to my family and friends, who have provided unwavering support throughout my writing journey. Your encouragement, patience, and love have been indispensable in helping me see this project through to completion.

Furthermore, I would like to extend my heartfelt thanks to my editor, whose expertise and guidance have been invaluable in shaping this book into its final form. Your insightful comments and meticulous attention to detail have significantly strengthened this work.

I am also deeply thankful to the numerous experts and professionals who generously contributed their time and shared their knowledge with me. Your perspectives and insights have enriched this book and made it even more compelling.

Secondly, I would like to acknowledge and express my gratitude to all those who played a significant role in bringing this book to life. From the web page designer, application designer, book cover designer, and everyone else whom I may have inadvertently omitted, thank you so much.

Finally, I wish to express my appreciation to the readers of this book, whose interest and engagement continue to inspire me to explore new ideas and share them with the world. Your feedback and support are incredibly valuable and mean everything to me.

This book has been a long and rewarding journey, and I could not have achieved it without the help of so many wonderful people. Once again, thank you from the bottom of my heart.

About the Author

MEET THE AUTHOR, A true Californian at heart who was born and raised in the Inland Empire of Southern California. Growing up in a vibrant and diverse community, this author developed a deep appreciation for hard work, dedication, and family values that would guide him throughout his life.

At the age of 17, this author signed up for the U.S. Army, eager to serve their country and make a difference in the world. He quickly discovered that military service was not just a job but a way of life that would help shape his character and instill in him a sense of purpose and responsibility.

After completing his service, this author continued his career in public service, working for a total of 17 years in the Veterans Health Administration (VHA) and Veterans Benefits Administration (VBA). Through his work, he saw firsthand the challenges and struggles that many veterans face and became passionate about advocating for their rights and ensuring they receive the support they deserve.

Throughout all of their experiences, the driving force behind this author's dedication and hard work has been their beautiful family. He has always strived to provide for his loved ones and create a better future for them, no matter the obstacles faced. Now, as an author, he brings all of his life experiences and values to his writing. With a deep appreciation for the power of storytelling, this author hopes to inspire others to persevere, overcome adversity, and find their own sense of purpose and fulfillment.

While working for a veteran hospital, he went from GS4 to GS6 and then became a GS10 with VBA as a Veterans Service Representative. Below are the jobs he worked with VHA and VBA:

- File Clerk
- Records Clerk
- Eligibility Clerk
- ER department

- Admissions
- Pre-Op/Post-Op
- Decedent Affairs

Furthermore, the author holds several certifications, including:

- Certified VBA
- Certified VHA
- Certified Advanced Peer Support Specialists
- Certified AHIMA Anatomy and Physiology
- Certified Medical Terminology

These certifications demonstrate his dedication and expertise in serving the veteran community.

Chapter 1: VHA Hospitals

———

HI, MY FELLOW MILITARY brothers and sisters from the past, present, and future! I am a vet myself, and the purpose of this chapter is to help you understand the different steps you can take to become a VHA patient. I was not aware of these tips and guidelines when I was in the military myself, and as a result, I had to go through quite a bit of struggle. My goal is to share my experience with others so that they don't face the same difficulties that I did.

First and foremost, as you may very well know, in order to become a VHA patient, you need to have been given an honorable or general discharge. A dishonorable discharge deems you ineligible to qualify as a VHA patient.

What are the different ways through which you can ensure that you do not receive a dishonorable discharge? Well, there are several important points you must keep in mind.

The most important thing is to always follow the orders given to you. Always. Remember that this is not college or high school, and there is little chance of you being able to get away with breaking the rules.

The second most important thing to note is that you must never go AWOL, no matter how pressing the need is or how short the duration of your absence is. For the uninitiated, AWOL stands for *Absence Without Official Leave*. Doing something like this might put your future in serious jeopardy because, a lot of times, the military doesn't immediately give a dishonorable discharge to enlisted candidates who have gone AWOL. Instead, what leadership does is wait till a serviceman has a couple of days left on their term before dishonorably discharging them. Thus, such a person can spend their entire time in the military believing that they'll be honorably discharged at the end while being woefully unaware of how they've already sabotaged their own future. Yes, I've seen problematic veterans receive a dishonorable discharge a few days shy of their completion date, pretty much as a form of payback for being so disruptive. Don't get taught this lesson.

In the unfortunate instance where you do happen to get a general discharge despite your best efforts, call the VA line at 1800-827-1000 for further assistance and inquire about the procedure needed to convert a dishonorable discharge into an honorable one. If you happen to receive a dishonorable discharge, there is still hope that you can apply to have your dishonorable discharge upgraded to a general discharge for VA benefits. A general discharge is not the same as an honorable discharge, but a general discharge can help a veteran obtain some benefits, which is better than having no benefits at all.

At this point, in case some readers need more encouragement, it might be apt to mention the numerous benefits that an honorable discharge carries.

- The first benefit that you gain from an honorable discharge is the VA Disability Compensation benefit. If you incurred a disability in the line of duty and were then honorably discharged, you can apply for up to 100% VA disability compensation, depending on the nature and severity of your disability. For a veteran who lives alone or has zero dependents, this compensation can be as much as $3600 per month. However, in order to qualify for this compensation, you must meet the following criteria:
- The disability must have been incurred in the line of duty.
- The condition must be at least 10% disabling, according to the VA's ratings.
- The disability must not have been caused by your own intentional misconduct.
- Your disability must be active, as seen through recurring symptoms.
- Another benefit that you gain is access to VA Healthcare. This is a comprehensive form of medical compensation that partially covers the costs of medical care, mental health treatments, substance abuse treatments, specialized care for women veterans, geriatrics and extended care, rehabilitation services, and much more. Although this benefit makes VA Healthcare much more affordable, keep in mind that you'll still need to co-pay to avail of any service. Co-pays are waived with a service-connected VA rating of 50% or higher or for veterans who can't afford to pay for VA healthcare.

- VA Educational Benefits are one of the greatest advantages of being honorably discharged. They are delivered through two bills: the Montgomery GI Bill and the Post-9/11 GI Bill.

The Post-9/11 GI Bill covers 100% of tuition costs for in-state public schools and includes an allowance for accommodation, books, supplies, and a one-time payment for relocation. With this benefit, veterans also qualify for vocational training, on-the-job training, internships, and flight training.

To be able to qualify for the complete list of benefits, at least one of the following criteria must be met:

- Veterans must have completed at least 36 months of active duty after September 10, 2001.
- Veterans must have received a Purple Heart with an honorable discharge; this allows them to bypass income requirements.
- The cause of discharge must be related to a service-connected disability, and veterans must have served for at least 30 days.

On the other hand, the Montgomery GI Bill pays up to $2210 per month for 2023 while veterans are enrolled in full-time school. This benefit can be availed for 36 months.

In order to be eligible for the Montgomery Bill, at least one of the following conditions must be fulfilled:

- The veteran contributed $100 per month for the first year of active service or qualified under VEAP conversion.
- The veteran graduated from high school or has an equivalency certificate.
- The veteran completed at least two years of active duty.
- An honorable discharge also supplies you with home loan benefits, so you can apply for a VA-supported home loan. The VA provides you with a portion of the loan, and this way, it eliminates the need for down payments and/or lowers mortgage insurance premiums. To be eligible for this benefit, veterans must have completed at least 90 days of active

duty during wartime or 24 consecutive months.

- The final benefit that I will be discussing here relates to VA employment and job training. The most difficult challenge that veterans face after being discharged is transitioning into regular civilian life. The VA Career Counseling program helps veterans in this regard by assisting them in figuring out what they want to do next in their lives. Counseling is offered in various formats, such as one-on-one counseling, group mentoring, workshops, etc. Veterans receive help with creating an effective resume, learning employable skills, and choosing an appropriate career path.

Let's move on to the next step. Once you've received your general or honorable discharge, the next step is to go to the nearest VA hospital at least 30 days before your term is supposed to end. And when you go there, make sure you take your DD 214 (Discharge Documents) with you because the officials won't just take you at your word. You will need to pre-register if you don't have your DD 214 documents with you, and you can come back to the VA once you receive them because your application will still be in pending status.

Apart from that, in order to apply, you'll also need your own social security number, as well as your spouse's and any qualified dependents' numbers. Additionally, you'll also need to carry with you an insurance card that provides information regarding all of the insurance companies that cover you, including any coverage that is given through a spouse, family member, or any other individual. This list includes Medicare, private insurance, and/or insurance from your employer.

The next item you need with you is your gross household income statement for the previous fiscal year for you, your spouse, and/or any other dependents. Gross income refers to the income allocated to you before any deductions take place, such as tax deductions, etc.

Lastly, you need to carry with you your deductible expenses for the past year. These include both education as well as healthcare costs.

At this point, it is best that I tell you about the importance your income plays in your potential selection as a VHA Patient. If you're making too much money, then your chances of selection are somewhat diminished. Alternatively, if you're a Purple Heart, then your chances of selection are greater than average, and if you have service connections, preferably 10% or more, then that too makes you more likely to be selected.

Next, let's look at the minimum duty requirements that make you eligible to apply for a VHA Patient.

Veterans who enlisted after September 7, 1980, or were drafted for active duty after October 16, 1981, must have completed at least 24 consecutive months, or the entire duration of the term for which they were called for active duty, in order to qualify.

However, these requirements do not apply to veterans who were discharged due to a disability or an aggravated injury inflicted while in the line of duty, nor do they apply to those who were discharged for hardships or received an *early discharge.*

These are only some of the exceptions to the minimum duty criteria, and since there are many others, the Veteran Administration encourages all veterans to apply in order to determine their eligibility. I, too, would urge you to do the same.

Now, let's briefly discuss how you can apply for a VHA Patient position.

There are four routes you can take. The first is to call the VHA hotline at 877-222-8387 for help. Their usual active hours are from 8:00 AM to 8:00 PM, Mondays through Fridays.

Alternatively, you can also apply by mail. This includes filling out an application for health benefits. You can access this application online. Once the form has been filled out, it must be signed and dated either by you or by the individual acting as your Power of Attorney. If you have taken the latter option, then you must also submit a copy of the Power of Attorney along with your Benefits application.

If you are signing the form yourself with an 'X,' then two other people must stand as witnesses to your signature, and their names and signatures will also need to be included in the application.

Once the form has been completed, you must post it to the following address:

Health Eligibility Center,

2957 Clairmont Rd., Suite 200,

Atlanta, GA 30329.

The third and final option is to apply *in-person*. Like before, you must first fill out the Health Benefits application and then sign it yourself or have it signed by someone acting as your Power of Attorney. Once done, the form has to be taken to the nearest VA medical center or clinic, where trained personnel will further guide you through the rest of the process.

The fourth option is perhaps the simplest. You can just send your application to the nearest VA Hospital and wait for them to contact you.

By this time, most readers might be wondering the same thing: how long does it take for an application status to be updated? As a general rule, a positive or negative decision is made on the spot, but if there are any further requirements, it takes around a week. If you haven't heard back during that time, do not apply again and instead call the VA Hotline at the same number that was provided above.

Before concluding, I would like to pass on a final message to those young readers who still haven't joined the military but hope to do so one day. To them, I would strongly advise that they not participate in any strenuous exercises or physically demanding sports that pose a risk to their bodies. Remember, if you enlist in the military with a torn ACL or a broken hip, they'll see you as a liability. The military prefers for recruits to be in as close to perfect health as possible in order for them to get the most use out of their services.

Chapter 2: VBA Regional Office

WHEN IT COMES TO SORTING out your veteran claims, you will need to visit a regional office. Unfortunately, regional offices are a bit like fast-food chains in the sense that they may all belong to the same corporation, but the standard of quality that you get in each office varies.

It is extremely important that you find out which regional offices have good ratings and which have bad ratings. This may require you to put in some effort, but the benefits will be worth it, as otherwise, you will not be adequately compensated for your disabilities. Remember, if the regional office is not to your liking and is not handling your claim in the manner that you desire, then it might be time to get your claim into the hands of another regional office. All of our time is important.

So, how can you determine which regional office will be favorable toward you and which will simply cause you more trouble than ease? In case you were wondering, no, you do not start calling up the various offices and asking them whether they're good or bad. Instead, what you want to do is contact the local veterans in your area and then consult them for help. These veterans will be able to better inform you regarding the ratings of various regional offices in your area.

What happens once you've finally identified a regional office with high ratings? Well, your work isn't done yet. Next, you'll need to determine whether you fall under that regional office's jurisdiction. This is dependent on your current address. The most likely scenario is that the regional office closest to you is probably the one whose jurisdiction you're living within. And if that regional office isn't good enough, then you might want to consider moving. Ratings can be figured out by speaking with other veterans about their experiences with their particular regional office. Regional offices with low ratings can take several years—in fact, as many as twenty in some cases—to process benefits, whereas higher-rated regional offices generally have a turn-around time ranging from three to twelve months. I know the prospect of shifting homes isn't an appealing one for anyone, but you might just want to consider doing it because otherwise, you risk jeopardizing your hard-earned benefits.

Next, let's discuss the documentation that you will need. Remember, having the correct documents with you is key to having your disability benefits processed on time. There are three primary documents that you should make sure to bring with you to the regional office.

The first document will be an honorable discharge DD-214 and military medical records to support the fact that your injuries indeed happened during service. The second document will be your current medical records, showing that the problem still hinders you from living a normal life. The third set of documents will be a letter from your physician stating that, in their opinion, your current problem is indeed originating from your time spent in service, and this will help to link everything together. The first document is an evidence letter showing that your disability is an in-service problem, the second document is your current records after you were out of service, and the third document is a provisional statement. The provisional statement can be especially helpful for you since it is a letter confirming that your problem started during your service years, and it lists the various symptoms and ailments that came about as a result of it.

Additionally, you can also bring a DBQ with you if you really want the process to turn out in your favor. A DBQ is a Disability Benefits Questionnaire, and it highlights in detail the nature and extent of your disabilities. One important thing to be cognizant of, however, is that you must always make sure that you have the right DBQ. In circumstances like this, it is crucial that you be specific. DBQ forms will need to be signed by your physician, whether that is a VA physician or an outside physician.

For example, if you are suffering from PTSD, you need to get a PTSD DBQ and not one similar to it, such as a DBQ for depression and/or anxiety. Similarly, if you're suffering from problems in your lower back, then get a DBQ that *exactly* mentions that, i.e., a lumbar DBQ, and not one that comes close, e.g., a cervical DBQ.

You can access the DBQ forms at this address: *Benefits.va.go*

There is one last thing I would like to mention on this front concerning disabilities. If you have a mental health disability, then make sure that you're displaying physical symptoms that are characteristic of that ailment. For example, if you're suffering from PTSD, don't walk into a hospital and begin sucking your thumb and acting like a five-year-old. Chances are, if you're doing that, you're either suffering from some other psychological disorder or, more likely, you're just trying to fool the system. Both possibilities don't bode well for you. Instead, make sure that your illness has been properly diagnosed and that the physical symptoms you are exhibiting are in line with the diagnosis.

Before concluding, I would like to mention some final tips that will prove helpful for those veterans suffering from a host of different disabilities. For such people, when they're submitting a disability form, it would be better if they just mentioned 3–4 ailments from their entire list of disabilities and then waited for those to be processed first before moving onto the next few. This way, you ensure that the turnaround time is significantly reduced and that you receive your disability benefits much sooner. Submitting ten, or even more than ten, disabilities at once only serves to overwhelm the Veteran's Service Representatives who are working on your case, and this ultimately delays your case further.

Suppose you have a list of the following disability symptoms:

1. Migraine
2. Sinus infection
3. Back pain
4. Neck pain
5. Ankle pain
6. Hair loss
7. Migraine
8. Sinus infection
9. Back Pain

Instead of sending in this entire list at once, it would be far better to break it down into portions, as shown below:

1. Neck pain
2. Ankle pain
3. Hair loss

Once the shorter list has been processed, you can then send in the next three conditions and so on.

Additionally, when submitting your form, you need to make sure that you have documentation of your medical history to support your claim.

If you have been given a 100% service-related disability, this means that you have a disabling condition that is directly related to your military service, and this disability has been classified as 100% disabling by the VA.

First of all, to those who have been awarded this, congratulations on this recognition of your service and sacrifice.

Secondly, there are certain steps you can take to ensure that the process goes as smoothly for you as possible. I have mentioned these steps below:

First and foremost, you'll want to review the decision letter that was awarded to you so that you understand the reasoning behind the decision as well as its effective date.

Secondly, make sure that you fully understand your benefits. A 100% service-related disability entitles you to a diverse range of benefits, including but not limited to medical care, compensation, education and training, and vocational rehabilitation. Make sure that you fully understand how all of these benefits work and how you can avail of them.

The next step is to consider financial planning. A 100% service-related disability award makes you eligible for tax-free disability compensation handed out by the VA. Consider consulting with a financial advisor, preferably one who is VA-accredited, so you can make safer and smarter plans for your future.

Since disability benefits are primarily concerned with providing medical treatment, let's now briefly discuss that. The important point to note is that even if you have been awarded a 100% service-related disability, it is crucial that you continue receiving medical treatment for your condition. The VA provides medical care for eligible veterans, so consider seeking treatment from a VA medical center or community provider. You are free to seek health care from outside physicians as well. Alternatively, there's nothing wrong with seeking a second opinion or just going to a physician who is more sympathetic to your needs. Use the health care system that gives you the care you're looking for.

If you are interested in or thinking about rejoining the workforce, then consider joining a vocational rehabilitation program. These programs ease your transition into the professional world by helping you develop skills, build an effective resume, and reach out to various suitable workplaces where you can find employment.

Finally, always try to remain connected with other veterans, as this is a great way to share your experiences, learn about new opportunities and resources, and be a part of a network that provides social and psychological support. If you're interested, you can even join a local veteran's organization or simply connect with other veterans online.

In summary, a 100% disability-related award offers numerous benefits and opportunities, and the resources that are made accessible to you depend on your own unique situation. If you are still confused and need more guidance, you can always speak to a Veteran Representative or a Veteran Service Organization that will give you more personalized advice and support.

Chapter 3: Benefits

———

MANY VETERANS COMPLETE their service and transition back to civilian life without realizing the full extent of benefits available to them. This chapter aims to shed light on the lesser-known benefits that can greatly enhance a veteran's quality of life. These benefits include car modifications, service animals, emotional support, tax reductions for health, student loan forgiveness, insurance, small business loans, home loans, and adaptive housing.

Education Benefits: The GI Bill

ONE OF THE MOST SIGNIFICANT benefits available to veterans is the GI Bill. The Post-9/11 GI Bill provides monthly financial assistance to help cover tuition costs and living expenses, allowing veterans to pursue a range of educational opportunities, including undergraduate and graduate degrees, vocational training, and certifications. This benefit not only reduces the financial burdens of pursuing higher education but also increases the chances of being accepted into a school or program due to the guaranteed funding provided to the institution.

The Post-9/11 GI Bill also offers additional benefits, such as the Yellow Ribbon Program, which helps cover the cost of tuition and fees at private schools and out-of-state public schools that might otherwise exceed the standard GI Bill funding limits. Furthermore, veterans can transfer their unused GI Bill benefits to eligible family members, including spouses and children, providing them with financial support to advance their education.

The Montgomery GI Bill is another tuition assistance program designed for veterans who served before September 10, 2001. It offers financial support for educational and training programs, including college degrees, vocational certifications, and on-the-job training. However, it is worth exploring whether converting to the post-9/11 GI Bill would yield more financial support, as it often provides more extensive benefits and greater flexibility in terms of eligible programs and institutions.

When considering GI Bill benefits, veterans should research the various educational programs available and weigh the pros and cons of each option. In some cases, it may be more advantageous to pursue vocational training or certifications that lead to in-demand, well-paying jobs. In other cases, a traditional college degree may be the best path to achieving career goals. Whichever path a veteran chooses, the GI Bill is an invaluable resource that can help ease the financial burden and open doors to new opportunities.

Vocational Rehabilitation: A Path to New Opportunities

VOCATIONAL REHABILITATION is an essential program for veterans who need to change career paths due to service-related injuries or disabilities. This program, often referred to as Voc Rehab or Chapter 31, offers comprehensive support to help veterans transition into a new field and regain their independence in the workforce.

Job Training and Education

VOCATIONAL REHABILITATION focuses on providing individualized job training and education tailored to the veteran's unique needs and goals. The program evaluates the veteran's skills, interests, and abilities and helps them identify suitable career options based on their specific circumstances. The training and education offered can include college or vocational school programs, on-the-job training, apprenticeships, and non-paid work experiences. In addition to covering tuition and fees, the program may also provide a monthly living stipend to eligible veterans during their training or education.

Career Counseling and Support Services

VETERANS PARTICIPATING in the vocational rehabilitation program also have access to career counseling and support services. This assistance can include resume development, job search assistance, interview coaching, and networking opportunities. These services aim to empower veterans by providing them with the tools and resources they need to secure meaningful employment.

Assistive Technology and Accommodations

IN SOME CASES, VETERANS may require assistive technology, adaptive equipment, or workplace accommodations to perform their new job effectively. The vocational rehabilitation program can provide financial assistance for these essential tools, such as specialized computer software, ergonomic office equipment, or other adaptive devices. Additionally, the program can help identify and coordinate any necessary workplace accommodations, ensuring that veterans can succeed in their new careers.

The vocational rehabilitation program is a valuable resource for veterans facing career changes due to service-related injuries or disabilities. By offering job training, education, and supportive services, the program helps veterans overcome obstacles and achieve their full potential in the workforce. With the right support, veterans can find meaningful employment, regain their independence, and enjoy a fulfilling life after military service.

Healthcare, Dental, and Mental Health Benefits: Comprehensive Care for Veterans

ACCESS TO QUALITY HEALTHCARE, dental, and mental health services is crucial for veterans adjusting to life after service. The Department of Veterans Affairs (VA) offers a range of benefits to address these needs and ensure veterans receive the care they deserve.

Healthcare Benefits

VA HEALTHCARE BENEFITS offer comprehensive medical coverage to eligible veterans, including preventive care, primary care, hospital services, and prescription medications. Depending on the veteran's eligibility, the copay for these services can be minimal or even free. To access VA healthcare, veterans must enroll in the program and may need to meet specific eligibility criteria, such as a minimum service duration or a service-connected disability rating.

Dental Benefits

DENTAL CARE CAN BE costly, but VA dental benefits can help offset these expenses for eligible veterans. Coverage can range from preventive services, such as cleanings and exams, to more complex treatments, such as root canals or dental implants. Veterans with service-connected dental issues may be eligible for comprehensive dental care at no cost. To access dental benefits, veterans must meet specific eligibility criteria and may need to enroll in the VA dental program.

Mental Health Benefits

MENTAL HEALTH SUPPORT is a vital aspect of a veteran's overall well-being. The VA offers a range of mental health services to address conditions such as PTSD, anxiety, depression, and chronic adjustment disorder. These services can include individual or group counseling, medication management, and specialized programs tailored to the unique needs of veterans. Access to mental health support can help veterans navigate the challenges of transitioning to civilian life and connect with other veterans who share similar experiences.

Disability Benefits and Compensation

VETERANS WITH SERVICE-related injuries or disabilities may be eligible for disability compensation, which provides a monthly tax-free payment. The amount of compensation depends on the severity of the disability and is determined by the VA's disability rating system. In addition to the compensation for the veteran, dependency benefits can provide extra financial support for the veteran's spouse, children, or dependent parents. These additional payments can help alleviate the financial burden on families and improve their overall quality of life. Healthcare, dental, and mental health benefits, along with disability compensation, play a crucial role in supporting veterans' well-being and financial stability after completing their service. By taking advantage of these benefits, veterans can access essential care and resources that can make a significant difference in their lives.

Home Loan Benefits and Adapted Housing Grants: Expanding Housing Opportunities for Veterans

VA Home Loans

THE VA NO-NO HOME LOAN, also known as the VA Loan, is a mortgage program designed specifically for veterans, active-duty service members, and their families. With no down payment or closing costs required, the VA Loan enables eligible borrowers to purchase a home more easily. This government-backed loan program also offers competitive interest rates, more flexible credit requirements, and no private mortgage insurance (PMI) obligations. To take advantage of the VA Loan, veterans must obtain a Certificate of Eligibility (COE) from the Department of Veterans Affairs.

Adapted Housing Grants

FOR VETERANS WITH SERVICE-related disabilities, adapted housing grants provide financial assistance to modify their homes and enhance accessibility. These grants can be used to install ramps, widen doorways, build walk-in bathtubs, modify kitchens, or add other accessibility features to the home. Two primary grant programs are available: the Specially Adapted Housing (SAH) Grant and the Special Housing Adaptation (SHA) Grant. Each program has specific eligibility criteria, and veterans must apply through the VA to access these funds.

Employment Benefits and Small Business Loans: Boosting Veteran Employment and Entrepreneurship

Veteran Employment Preference

VETERANS RECEIVE PREFERENCE in the hiring process for federal government positions, giving them an advantage over civilian candidates. This preference can be applied to both competitive and non-competitive hiring processes, depending on the veteran's qualifications and the type of job. In some cases, veterans with disabilities may be eligible for a non-competitive appointment, bypassing the traditional application process altogether.

Small Business Loans

FOR VETERANS INTERESTED in starting their own businesses, small business loan programs are available that cater specifically to their needs. The Small Business Administration (SBA) offers resources such as the Veterans Advantage Loan Program, which provides lower fees and streamlined application processes for veterans seeking business financing. By taking advantage of these programs, veterans can access capital to launch and grow their businesses, creating new employment opportunities for themselves and others.

Additional Benefits: Enhancing Quality of Life for Veterans

Emotional Support and Service Dogs

EMOTIONAL SUPPORT DOGS and service dogs can make a significant difference in the lives of veterans with disabilities or mental health challenges. Service dogs are specially trained to perform tasks for individuals with specific disabilities, such as guiding visually impaired individuals or retrieving items for those with mobility impairments. Emotional support dogs provide companionship and emotional support, which can be particularly beneficial for veterans dealing with PTSD or anxiety. Veterans can apply for a service dog through various organizations or consult with their healthcare provider about acquiring an emotional support dog.

For information on service dogs, follow the website below:

https://veteran.com/service-dogs/

And for information on emotional support dogs, head to the website below:

Therapypet.org[1]

Handicapped Placard and Vehicle Registration Exemptions

VETERANS WITH SERVICE-related mobility issues may qualify for a handicapped placard for their vehicle. This placard allows them to park in designated handicapped spaces, making it easier to access facilities and services. In some states, veterans with a handicapped placard or specialized license plates may also be eligible for vehicle registration exemptions or reduced fees, providing additional financial relief.

By leveraging these home loan benefits, adapted housing grants, employment benefits, and additional resources, veterans can improve their quality of life and access essential support during their transition to civilian life. Understanding and utilizing these lesser-known benefits can significantly improve the quality of life for military veterans. By spreading awareness of these resources, veterans can access the support they need and deserve after serving their country.

---

1. http://therapypet.org/

Chapter 4: Networking

NETWORKING AMONG VETERANS is crucial, as it enables us to connect with others who understand the unique challenges we face. The benefits available to us can be like an Easter egg hunt—scattered around and hard to find. Two veterans leaving the service at different times and locations may receive vastly different information on the benefits available to them.

Some veterans may be lucky enough to have someone who cares enough to provide them with the necessary information and resources. Others may be handed a stack of pamphlets and left to figure it out on their own. That's why it's important to speak with other veterans and compare each other's experiences.

As veterans transition from military to civilian life, there are many challenges to overcome. One of the biggest hurdles can be finding meaningful employment and building relationships in a new community. That's why networking is so important for veterans. It can help us find job opportunities, build relationships with peers and mentors, and gain support in our civilian lives.

I know firsthand how difficult it can be to adjust to civilian life after serving in the military. I spent years in the Army, where I had a tight-knit community of fellow soldiers who understood my experiences and shared my values. When I left the military, I felt adrift and disconnected. I needed to figure out where to turn for help or support.

That's when I discovered the power of networking. By reaching out to other veterans and professionals in my field, I was able to build a new community and find new opportunities. Through networking, I was able to land a job I love, connect with mentors who have helped me grow professionally, and build relationships with fellow veterans who understand my experiences.

In this chapter, we'll explore the importance of networking for veterans and offer tips and strategies for effective networking. We'll also discuss the various resources and opportunities available to veterans, including those provided by the Department of Veterans Affairs and other organizations. Whether you're a recent veteran or you've been out of the military for years, networking can be a powerful tool for building connections and achieving success in your civilian life.

Through networking, we can share information and learn from each other's experiences. We can ask questions and find out what benefits we may be eligible for. We can compare our out-processing experiences and help each other avoid the pitfalls of the transition from military to civilian life.

For example, through networking, I learned that I could file a claim for benefits up to three months before leaving the service. This allowed me to have money waiting for me on the day I got out, making for a much smoother transition. It's critical to have some form of income when leaving the service to avoid falling into financial hardship.

By networking, we can access resources and support that can make all the difference in our transition to civilian life. So, my fellow veterans, don't hesitate to reach out to others and build those connections. It's a must-do to ensure a successful transition to civilian life.

The Benefits of Networking for Veterans

AS VETERANS, WE BRING a unique set of skills and experiences to the table. However, transitioning to civilian life can be a daunting task, and we may face challenges that our civilian peers do not. That's where networking can help.

Networking offers a range of benefits for veterans. First and foremost, it can help us find job opportunities. By building relationships with professionals in our desired fields, we can learn about job openings and get inside information on what employers are looking for.

In addition to job opportunities, networking can help us build relationships with peers and mentors. This is especially important for veterans, who may feel isolated or disconnected from civilian life. By connecting with other veterans and professionals, we can build a sense of community and find others who share our values and experiences.

Networking also provides access to resources and support. Whether it's learning about education and training programs, accessing healthcare resources, or finding financial support, networking can connect us with the resources we need to succeed.

Tips for Effective Networking

WHILE NETWORKING CAN offer a range of benefits for veterans, it's not always easy to know where to start. Here are some tips to help you network effectively:

1. Identify potential contacts: Think about the people you know, both inside and outside the military, who might be able to help you. This could include former colleagues, friends, family members, or even strangers you meet at networking events.
2. Be prepared: Before you reach out to potential contacts, make sure you have a clear idea of what you're looking for. Are you seeking job opportunities, mentorship, or support? Having a clear goal in mind will help you focus your networking efforts.
3. Attend networking events: Look for networking events in your area, including job fairs, professional conferences, and community events. These events can provide valuable opportunities to meet new people and make connections.
4. Follow up: After making a new connection, be sure to follow up with a 'thank you' email or message. This can help solidify the relationship and keep you at the top of their mind for future opportunities.

Personally, I've found that networking can be challenging at times, particularly when I feel shy or uncertain about how to approach new contacts. However, I've also learned that practicing my networking skills can help me feel more confident and prepared.

One strategy that has worked well for me is to practice my networking skills with peers or mentors. This can help me refine my approach and get feedback on how to improve.

Another approach is to seek support from VA programs or counseling services. These resources can provide valuable guidance on how to network effectively, as well as emotional support and encouragement.

Ultimately, the key to effective networking is to be open, curious, and persistent. By building relationships with others and seeking out new opportunities, we can find success in our civilian lives.

Networking Opportunities for Veterans

AS VETERANS, WE HAVE access to a range of networking opportunities. Here are some of the most common options:

1. Job fairs: Many organizations and employers host job fairs specifically for veterans. These events can provide valuable opportunities to connect with potential employers and learn about job openings.
2. Professional organizations: There are many professional organizations that cater to veterans and offer networking opportunities. These organizations can provide access to resources and support, as well as the chance to connect with peers and mentors.
3. Community groups: Local community groups, such as veteran service organizations or volunteer groups, can also provide valuable networking opportunities. These groups often have a strong sense of community and can offer support and guidance to veterans in need.
4. Online networking: In today's digital age, online networking can be a powerful tool. Platforms like LinkedIn can provide a way to connect with professionals in your desired field, learn about job openings, and

build relationships with others.

1. Connect with Fellow Service Members at VA Hospitals: One of the most significant benefits of being a veteran is the camaraderie and brotherhood that come with serving in the military. As a patient at a VA hospital, you have a unique opportunity to connect with other veterans and share your experiences.

It's not uncommon for veterans from different time periods to run into each other while at a VA hospital, often leading to unexpected reunions and chance encounters. You may find yourself striking up conversations and swapping stories with fellow service members who share a common bond.

These conversations can provide a valuable opportunity to catch up with old friends, make new connections, and even network for potential job opportunities. In addition to the social benefits, connecting with other veterans can also provide a sense of comfort and understanding, especially for those dealing with physical or mental health issues related to their time in service.

I've personally witnessed many heartwarming surprise reunions between veterans from the Vietnam era of 1954 to 1974 while they were visiting VA hospitals. These chance encounters not only provide an opportunity to catch up on old times but also offer a chance to network and potentially make connections that could lead to new opportunities.

Personally, I've found that attending job fairs and networking events is a great way to connect with potential employers and build relationships with peers and mentors. I've also found online networking to be helpful, particularly when it comes to learning about job opportunities.

In addition to these resources, it's important to note that many VA programs and organizations offer networking opportunities for veterans. These resources can provide valuable guidance and support, as well as access to job training programs, financial assistance, and healthcare resources.

By taking advantage of these resources, veterans can build strong networks and find success in their civilian lives.

Overcoming Networking Challenges

WHILE NETWORKING CAN be a powerful tool for veterans, it's not always easy to put ourselves out there and make new connections. Here are some common challenges veterans may face when networking, along with strategies for overcoming them:

Shyness or introversion: If you're shy or introverted, networking can feel overwhelming. One strategy is to start small and practice your networking skills with peers or mentors. You can also set small goals, such as attending one networking event per month, to help build your confidence over time.

Feeling disconnected: Veterans may feel disconnected from civilian life, which can make it hard to connect with others. One strategy is to seek out networking events and groups specifically for veterans, where you can meet others who share your experiences and values.

Lack of experience: If you're new to networking, it can be hard to know where to start. One strategy is to seek guidance from VA programs or other organizations that provide support and resources for veterans. You can also practice your networking skills with peers or mentors to build your confidence.

Personally, I've faced my share of networking challenges over the years. When I first left the military, I felt disconnected and uncertain about how to make new connections. However, I've found that practicing my networking skills and seeking out support from VA programs and other organizations has been incredibly helpful. By overcoming these challenges and building strong networks, veterans can find success in their civilian lives. Whether you're seeking employment, mentorship, or support, networking can provide a valuable tool for achieving your goals.

While networking can be challenging at times, it's important to remember that we're not alone. There are many resources and organizations available to support veterans in their networking efforts, from job fairs and professional organizations to VA programs and counseling services.

Personally, I've found that networking has been a critical part of my own success as a veteran. By building relationships with peers and mentors, I've been able to find new job opportunities, grow professionally, and connect with others who share my experiences and values.

As you embark on your own networking journey, remember that it's never too late to start. By setting goals, seeking support, and practicing your networking skills, you can build strong connections and find success in your civilian life.

Thank you for your service, and good luck with your networking efforts.

Chapter 5: Retirement

———

IT'S QUITE A UNIQUE experience to retire from the military in your late 30s. Not many people have the opportunity to retire this young, but for those of us in the military, it's not uncommon. Some even retire young due to medical reasons or because they enlisted at a very young age. This early retirement opens up the possibility of having a second career and retiring in the private sector.

Retirement Benefits in the Military

DURING MY TIME IN THE military, I learned about the various retirement benefits that I'd receive once I completed my service. These benefits can be a significant factor in one's decision to stay in the military for the long haul, and they have provided a solid foundation for veteran lives. Here are some of the key benefits you can enjoy upon retiring from the military:

1. Pension: The military pension is a significant part of the retirement package. It provides a monthly income based on a percentage of the service member's basic pay. The percentage is determined by the number of years served and the rank at the time of retirement. The pension is also adjusted for inflation, ensuring that the purchasing power of the monthly income remains relatively constant over time.

2. Health care: Access to quality health care is another major benefit of military retirement. As a retiree, you are eligible for the TRICARE health care program, which offers comprehensive coverage for you and your dependents. This coverage includes hospitalization, outpatient care, prescription medications, and more. The costs associated with TRICARE are generally lower than those of comparable civilian health insurance plans, making it a valuable benefit for retirees.

3. Education benefits: The military offers several education benefits, such as the Post-9/11 GI Bill, which can be used by retirees to further their education or transfer to their dependents. You can take advantage of this benefit to obtain a degree in a field that interests you, which greatly

improves your prospects for a second career in the private sector.

4. Commissary and exchange privileges: Retiring from the military can grant veterans lifetime access to commissaries and exchanges, where they can purchase groceries, household items, and other goods at reduced prices. This benefit helps them save money on everyday expenses and maintain a higher standard of living.

5. Base privileges: As a military retiree, one can also retain access to base amenities such as gyms, recreational facilities, and clubs. These facilities provide you with a sense of community and a place to socialize with other veterans and active-duty service members.

6. Space-Available Travel: Another perk of military retirement is the opportunity to travel on military aircraft when space is available. Although not guaranteed, Space-A travel can be a cost-effective way to explore new destinations, both domestically and internationally.

Despite these benefits, there are some disadvantages to military retirement that one may want to consider. One such drawback was the limitation on where you could live or work after retirement. Many of the job opportunities available to military retirees are concentrated around military bases, which may not always align with personal preferences for location or lifestyle. Additionally, transitioning to civilian life can be challenging, as the skills and experiences gained in the military may not always translate directly to the private sector.

The military pension system may not be as generous for those who served less than 20 years or did not attain a high rank. In these cases, the retirement benefits may not provide the same level of financial security as those offered by private sector employers, who often provide 401(k) plans or other investment vehicles.

Overall, veterans' military retirement benefits played a significant role in shaping their post-service lives. They provided them with financial stability, access to quality health care, and opportunities for personal growth through education and travel. However, it's essential to weigh these benefits against the potential limitations and challenges associated with military retirement and to plan accordingly for a successful transition to civilian life.

Medical Retirement in the Military

THROUGHOUT MY CAREER, I saw some of my fellow service members go through medical retirement. This occurs when a service member can no longer perform their duties due to a service-related injury or illness. The criteria for receiving medical retirement benefits are strict, and the process of applying can be lengthy and challenging. Here, I'll provide more details on the medical retirement process and the challenges faced by those seeking it.

1. Criteria for medical retirement: In order to qualify for medical retirement, a service member must be deemed *unfit for duty* due to a service-related injury or illness. This determination is made by a Medical Evaluation Board (MEB) and a Physical Evaluation Board (PEB), which evaluate the service member's medical condition and ability to perform their duties. The injury or illness must be severe enough to prevent the service member from fulfilling their military obligations and must have been sustained or aggravated during their time in service.

2. Disability rating: If the MEB and PEB find a service member unfit for duty, they will assign a disability rating based on the severity of the condition. This rating, expressed as a percentage, determines the level of benefits the service member will receive. In order to qualify for medical retirement, the disability rating must be at least 30%. Those with a lower rating may still receive some benefits, but they will be separated from the military rather than retired.

3. Benefits for medically retired service members: Medically retired service members receive a range of benefits, including a disability retirement pension that is calculated based on their disability rating and years of service. They also retain access to TRICARE health care coverage and other benefits available to military retirees, such as commissary and exchange privileges, base amenities, and Space-A travel.

4. Challenges in the medical retirement process: The process of applying for medical retirement can be lengthy, taking anywhere from several months to over a year. During this time, the service member may be placed on limited duty or assigned to a Warrior Transition Unit, where they receive medical treatment and support while awaiting the outcome

of their case. This period can be emotionally and financially challenging for service members and their families, as they face uncertainty about their future and a potential loss of income.

Medical retirement in the military is a complex process that requires service members to meet strict criteria and navigate a lengthy application process. Those who qualify for medical retirement receive a range of benefits, including a disability pension and health care coverage. However, they also face unique challenges in transitioning to civilian life, particularly if dealing with ongoing health issues. By understanding the medical retirement process and leveraging available resources, medically retired service members can better prepare for their future and overcome the challenges they may encounter.

Enlisting at a Young Age

IF YOU ENLIST IN THE military when you're just 18 years old, your decision shapes the course of your life in many ways. Joining the military at such a young age comes with a unique set of benefits and challenges that influence your personal and professional growth.

1. Benefits of enlisting at a young age:

a) Early retirement: One of the most significant advantages of enlisting at a young age is the potential for early retirement. After 20 years of service, veterans are able to retire at the age of 38 or sooner in some cases, granting them the opportunity to pursue a second career or enjoy an extended period of leisure.

b) Valuable life experience: Joining the military at 18 exposes you to a diverse array of experiences, cultures, and responsibilities that most of your peers do not encounter. This exposure helps you develop important life skills, such as leadership, discipline, and adaptability, which will serve you well in your post-military life.

c) Educational opportunities: The military offers various educational benefits, including tuition assistance and the GI Bill, which can be used to further one's education during or after service. By enlisting at a young age, I was able to take advantage of these opportunities earlier in life, setting the stage for a successful post-military career.

1. Challenges of enlisting at a young age:

a) Adapting to military life: The transition from civilian to military life can be challenging, especially for those who join at a young age. I had to quickly adapt to the strict discipline, regimented schedule, and hierarchical structure of the military, which required significant personal growth and adjustment.

b) Potential career limitations: Enlisting at a young age may limit one's career options within the military, as certain roles or advancement opportunities may be restricted by age, education, or experience. One may have to carefully plan their career progression and seek out additional training and education to overcome these limitations.

c) Personal sacrifices: Joining the military at 18 meant that I had to make personal sacrifices, such as spending extended periods away from family and friends and missing out on traditional milestones like attending college right after high school. The demands of military life can also put a strain on relationships and make it difficult to maintain a sense of stability.

d) Making the most of enlisting at a young age: Despite the challenges, I found that enlisting at a young age offered unique opportunities for personal and professional growth. By actively seeking out new experiences, pursuing education and training opportunities, and developing a strong support network, I was able to maximize the benefits of my early enlistment and build a successful military career that set the stage for a fulfilling post-military life.

Enlisting in the military at a young age presents both benefits and challenges. The opportunity for early retirement, valuable life experience, and educational opportunities can be significant advantages while adapting to military life, facing potential career limitations, and making personal sacrifices can be challenging. By recognizing and addressing these challenges, young service members can make the most of their military service and set themselves up for success in their post-military lives.

Retirement Planning

PLANNING FOR RETIREMENT is an essential part of a veteran's military career, as it allows them to transition into civilian life with financial stability and peace of mind. Throughout your service, you should take several steps to ensure your financial well-being and prepare for life after the military. Here are some of the key aspects of my retirement planning process:

1. Consultation with financial experts: Early in your career, seek advice from financial experts, such as military financial counselors and certified financial planners. They can help you understand your retirement benefits, develop a budget, and create a personalized financial plan. By working with these experts, you can make informed decisions about your finances and develop a roadmap for achieving your retirement goals.

2. Saving and investing: You should make it a priority to save and invest throughout your military career. Take advantage of the Thrift Savings Plan (TSP), a tax-advantaged retirement savings plans available to service members, and contribute a portion of your pay each month. Additionally, invest in other financial vehicles, such as individual retirement accounts (IRAs) and mutual funds, to diversify your investments and maximize the potential returns. Again, use your networking skills before investing in IRA/401(k) plans, as some can be scams.

3. Debt management: Managing debt is another crucial aspect of the retirement planning process. Focus on paying off high-interest debt, such as credit card balances, as quickly as possible and utilize low-

interest loans, like the VA home loan, when necessary. By minimizing your debt, you can allocate more of your income toward savings and investments.

4. Planning for a second career: As part of your retirement planning, also consider the possibility of pursuing a second career in the private sector. This involves identifying potential fields of interest, obtaining additional education or certifications, and networking with professionals in those industries. A second career can not only provide you with additional income but also offer the potential for additional retirement benefits.

5. Establishing an emergency fund: Throughout your military career, maintain an emergency fund with at least six months' worth of living expenses. This financial cushion provides you with peace of mind and allows you to handle unexpected expenses or financial challenges without jeopardizing your long-term financial goals.

6. Insurance planning: Ensuring adequate insurance coverage is another important aspect of the retirement planning process. Review your life insurance, disability insurance, and long-term care insurance regularly to ensure that you have sufficient coverage to protect yourself and your family in the event of unforeseen circumstances.

Retirement planning plays a crucial role in a military career and enables a smoother transition into civilian life with financial stability. By consulting with financial experts, saving and investing, managing debt, planning for a second career, establishing an emergency fund, and ensuring adequate insurance coverage, you can create a comprehensive financial plan that sets you up for success in your post-military life.

Retiring from the military at a young age has its benefits, such as the opportunity for a second career and competitive retirement benefits. However, it's essential to plan carefully for the future, including considering post-military employment and financial stability. Overall, military retirement can give you a chance to start a new chapter in life, and you can be grateful for the experiences and opportunities it provides.

Chapter 6: Death Benefits

―――

Overview of Dependency and Indemnity Compensation (DIC) program

THE SUDDEN AND TRAGIC loss of a loved one who served in the military is a heartbreaking and challenging experience for the surviving family members. Amidst the grief and emotional turmoil, financial burdens can add more stress to an already difficult situation. Recognizing the sacrifices made by veterans and their families, the U.S. government has established the Dependency and Indemnity Compensation (DIC) program to provide some relief and support during these challenging times.

Administered by the Department of Veterans Affairs (VA), the DIC program is a lifeline to the families left behind, offering tax-free financial assistance to eligible surviving spouses, children, and dependent parents. This vital support system honors the service and dedication of our fallen heroes and acknowledges the void left in their families' lives.

Purpose: provide tax-free financial assistance to surviving family members

WHEN A MILITARY VETERAN passes away, it is not uncommon for their loved ones to find themselves grappling with financial uncertainties. The DIC program seeks to alleviate these concerns by providing a tax-free financial cushion to help families cope with the loss and navigate the road ahead. The compensation, tailored to address the unique needs of each family, takes into account various factors such as the veteran's military service, cause of death, and other eligibility criteria.

The goal of the DIC program is to offer a safety net for those left behind, ensuring that they have the necessary resources to cover living expenses, medical bills, and other financial needs. It is a testament to the nation's gratitude and commitment to those who have served and their families. The program seeks to provide a sense of financial security and stability, allowing survivors the opportunity to heal and rebuild their lives without the added burden of financial stress.

In the coming sections, we will delve deeper into the specifics of the DIC program, exploring the different benefits available, eligibility requirements, and the application process. This comprehensive guide aims to empower and inform surviving family members of their rights and options, enabling them to access the full range of benefits they are entitled to and to honor the memory of their beloved veteran.

DIC Compensation

Factors affecting the amount

Military service of the deceased veteran

THE DIC PROGRAM TAKES into account the veteran's military service when determining the amount of compensation to be provided. Various aspects of the veteran's service record, such as their rank, time in service, and the nature of their duties, can influence the compensation amount. A higher rank or an extensive service history may result in a larger benefit for the surviving family members. This consideration acknowledges the dedication and commitment of the veteran to their country and the impact their service may have had on their families' lives.

Cause of death

THE CAUSE OF DEATH is another significant factor in determining the amount of DIC compensation. If the veteran's death is directly related to their military service, such as a result of injuries sustained in combat or service-connected health conditions, the compensation may be higher. This recognizes the direct link between the veteran's service and the family's loss and ensures that the survivors receive appropriate financial support in light of the ultimate sacrifice made by the veteran. It is to be noted that if the veteran's death is not service-related, the compensation may be lower. However, the DIC program still acknowledges the veteran's service and aims to provide financial assistance to their family, recognizing that the loss of a loved one is challenging, regardless of the cause of death.

Eligibility criteria

THE ELIGIBILITY CRITERIA for the DIC program are designed to ensure that the financial assistance reaches those who need it most. Various factors are considered when determining eligibility, such as the relationship of the survivor to the deceased veteran, whether the survivor is financially dependent on the veteran, and if the veteran's death was service-connected or not.

For instance, a surviving spouse may be eligible for compensation if they were married to the veteran at the time of the veteran's death, while a child may be eligible if they are under 18 or up to 23 if attending school. Dependent parents may also qualify if they can demonstrate financial dependence on the veteran. These criteria are in place to guarantee that the compensation is directed toward those who are most affected by the loss and are in need of support.

By taking these factors into account, the DIC program aims to provide a tailored and compassionate approach to supporting the families of deceased veterans. By understanding the unique circumstances surrounding each family's situation, the program can ensure that the financial assistance offered is both meaningful and impactful, helping survivors as they navigate through the difficult journey of healing and rebuilding their lives.

Monthly payment to cover

Living expenses

LOSING A LOVED ONE often comes with a myriad of emotional and financial challenges. The DIC program aims to provide some relief by offering a monthly payment designed to help cover living expenses such as housing, utilities, and groceries. This financial support is essential in enabling the surviving family members to maintain their daily lives and focus on the healing process.

As families adjust to life without their loved ones, they may face changes in their financial situation. The monthly DIC payment is intended to ease this transition, allowing them the necessary time and space to adapt and establish a new sense of normalcy. By addressing these fundamental living expenses, the program helps to create a stable environment in which survivors can grieve and heal without the constant worry of meeting their basic needs.

Medical bills

THE LOSS OF A LOVED one can sometimes be accompanied by medical expenses that may be overwhelming for the surviving family members. Whether it's the cost of the deceased veteran's medical care or the ongoing healthcare needs of the family, these expenses can place additional strain on an already difficult situation.

The monthly DIC payment can be used to help cover these medical bills, easing the financial burden and providing some peace of mind during a time of emotional turmoil. This support allows families to focus on their well-being and healing rather than becoming overwhelmed by medical expenses.

Other needs

IN ADDITION TO LIVING expenses and medical bills, families may face various other financial needs as they cope with the loss of their loved one. These needs could include funeral costs, educational expenses for children, or even transportation and childcare expenses for single-parent families.

The DIC program is designed to be flexible, allowing families to use the monthly payment to address these additional needs as they arise. This flexibility empowers survivors to prioritize their most pressing financial concerns and make decisions that best serve their individual circumstances. By addressing these diverse needs, the DIC program demonstrates its commitment to providing comprehensive support to the families of deceased veterans.

The monthly DIC payment is a vital lifeline for the families of veterans who have made the ultimate sacrifice for their country. By providing financial assistance to help cover living expenses, medical bills, and other needs, the program offers a helping hand to those left behind, allowing them the opportunity to grieve, heal, and rebuild their lives without the added stress of financial difficulties. As the surviving family members navigate through the complex and emotional journey of loss, the DIC program stands as a testament to our nation's gratitude and commitment to those who have served and their families.

Additional Benefits

Survivors' and Dependents' Educational Assistance (DEA) program

IN THE FACE OF A SIGNIFICANT loss, the surviving family members may find it difficult to envision their future, particularly when it comes to educational and career goals. With this in mind, the VA provides the Survivors' and Dependents' Educational Assistance (DEA) program, offering educational opportunities and financial aid to help them pursue their dreams.

The DEA program extends its support to eligible spouses, children, and dependents of deceased veterans, empowering them to further their education through various avenues such as college degrees, certificate programs, apprenticeships, or on-the-job training. By investing in the education and personal growth of the survivors, the program helps them build a brighter future for themselves and their families.

Survivors' pension programs

FINANCIAL STABILITY is essential for the well-being and long-term security of the surviving family members. In addition to the DIC program, the VA also offers survivor's pension programs that provide an extra layer of financial support to eligible dependents. These programs aim to ensure that the families left behind continue to receive adequate financial assistance, helping them maintain a sense of stability and security in the wake of their loss. Survivors' pension programs are designed to supplement the income of the surviving family members, as they offer a monthly payment to help them maintain a comfortable lifestyle. This financial support can be vital for families who may be struggling to make ends meet, providing a buffer that enables them to focus on their healing journey without the constant worry of financial difficulties.

Eligibility criteria and variations

THE AVAILABILITY AND extent of additional benefits, such as the DEA program and survivor's pension programs, depend on several factors, including the veteran's service history, length of service, and the relationship between the survivor and the deceased veteran. Understanding these eligibility criteria is crucial to ensuring that the surviving family members can access the full range of benefits to which they are entitled.

Eligibility for the DEA program, for instance, depends on the survivor's relationship to the deceased veteran, their age, and whether the veteran's death was service-connected. Similarly, for survivors' pension programs, factors such as the veteran's length of service, the survivor's income, and their relationship to the deceased veteran play a vital role in determining eligibility.

In order to maximize the benefits available to the surviving family members, it is essential to work with a qualified VA representative who can guide them through the process and help them understand their rights and options. By being well-informed and supported, survivors can make the most of the available benefits, providing a sense of financial security and hope as they navigate the emotional journey of loss and healing.

Working with a Qualified VA Representative

Importance of guidance for claiming benefits

THE PROCESS OF CLAIMING benefits can be complex and overwhelming, particularly for those who are grieving the loss of a loved one. Working with a qualified VA representative is essential as it allows the surviving family members to receive the full range of benefits to which they are entitled to. These representatives are trained professionals with extensive knowledge of the various programs and benefits offered by the VA, making them an invaluable resource for survivors navigating the system.

If you're searching for a qualified VA representative, your first step should be to visit the nearest VA hospital. Once there, simply make your way to the information desk and request to speak with someone from the Decedent Affairs or Death Benefits Department. I've found that the latter option flows more smoothly and is easier to recall. This department is staffed by knowledgeable VA representatives who can assist you with any questions you may have regarding veterans' benefits following the passing of a loved one.

A knowledgeable VA representative can help families understand the eligibility criteria, application process, and documentation required for each benefit program. They can also provide support in addressing any concerns or questions that may arise during the process. By guiding survivors through this intricate landscape, a VA representative can help alleviate some of the stress and confusion that often accompany the claim of benefits.

Understanding rights and options

IN ADDITION TO PROVIDING guidance on the application process, a VA representative can also help survivors understand their rights and options. This is crucial in ensuring that families are empowered to make informed decisions that best suit their unique circumstances and needs. By being well-informed about the available benefits, survivors can better advocate for themselves and secure the support they need during this challenging time.

A qualified VA representative can help identify potential benefits that a survivor might not have been aware of, such as educational assistance programs or additional pension support. They can also clarify any misconceptions or misunderstandings about the programs, ensuring that survivors have accurate information to make well-informed decisions.

Working with a qualified VA representative is an essential step in claiming the full range of benefits available to surviving family members of deceased veterans. Their guidance, support, and expertise can make the process more manageable, providing survivors with the tools they need to secure the financial assistance and support necessary to rebuild their lives. By understanding their rights and options, survivors can face the future with confidence and hope, honoring the memory of their loved ones while forging a path forward for themselves and their families.

Required Forms

Military Records Request: Form SF 180

TO INITIATE THE PROCESS of claiming benefits, survivors must first request the deceased veteran's military records. This can be done by submitting Form SF 180, the Military Records Request form. These records contain essential information about the veteran's service history, such as their rank, dates of service, and any service-connected disabilities. Obtaining these records is a crucial step in determining eligibility for various benefits and programs.

Application for Burial Benefits: Form 21P-530

THE VA PROVIDES BURIAL benefits to help cover the cost of funeral and burial expenses for eligible veterans. To apply for these benefits, survivors need to complete and submit Form 21P-530, the Application for Burial Benefits. This form helps the VA assess eligibility for burial benefits and determine the appropriate amount of financial assistance to be provided.

Claim for Standard Government Headstone or Marker: Form 40-1330

ELIGIBLE VETERANS MAY receive government-furnished headstones or markers for their graves at no cost to their families. To request a standard government headstone or marker, survivors must complete and submit Form 40-1330. This form provides the necessary information for the VA to process the request and ensure that the headstone or marker accurately reflects the veteran's service.

Presidential Memorial Certificate Request: Form 40-0247

THE PRESIDENTIAL MEMORIAL Certificate (PMC) is an engraved paper certificate signed by the current President, expressing the nation's gratitude for the deceased veteran's service. To request a PMC, survivors must complete and submit Form 40-0247, the Presidential Memorial Certificate Request Form. The PMC serves as a lasting symbol of recognition and appreciation for the veteran's service and sacrifice, providing a cherished memento for the family to honor their loved one's memory.

VA Funeral Expenses

Up to $700 for eligible service members

THE VA RECOGNIZES THE financial burden that funeral expenses can place on surviving family members and offers assistance to help alleviate some of the costs. For eligible service members who died while hospitalized at a VA facility or under VA-contracted care, the VA can provide up to $700 to cover funeral expenses. This financial support helps to ease the strain on the family during an emotionally challenging time, allowing them to focus on honoring their loved one's memory and navigating the grieving process.

VA does not provide caskets or urns

IT IS IMPORTANT TO note that the VA does not currently provide caskets or urns for the interment or inurnment of deceased veterans. While the VA does offer other funeral and burial benefits, such as headstones, markers, and financial assistance for eligible expenses, the cost of a casket or urn remains the responsibility of the family. As a result, it is essential for families to take this into consideration when planning and budgeting for their loved one's funeral arrangements.

Required Documents

Will

A WILL IS A LEGAL DOCUMENT outlining the deceased's wishes regarding the distribution of their assets and the care of any minor children. Having a copy of the will is essential to ensuring that the deceased's wishes are respected and carried out as intended. It may also provide valuable information when applying for VA benefits and navigating the legal processes following the veteran's death.

DD214

THE DD214, OR CERTIFICATE of Release or Discharge from Active Duty, is a crucial document that provides detailed information about the veteran's military service, such as their dates of service, rank, and any awards or citations received. This document is required when applying for various VA benefits, including burial benefits and survivor's pensions.

Advanced Directive

AN ADVANCED DIRECTIVE is a legal document that outlines the medical care preferences of an individual in the event they become unable to make their own healthcare decisions. Having a copy of the deceased veteran's advanced directive can provide valuable insight into their wishes regarding medical treatment and end-of-life care.

Durable Power of Attorney for Finance

A DURABLE POWER OF attorney for finance is a legal document that grants a designated individual the authority to manage the financial affairs of another person. In the case of a deceased veteran, having a copy of this document can help ensure a smooth transition of financial responsibilities and provide essential information when applying for benefits.

Living Trust

A LIVING TRUST IS A legal arrangement in which an individual's assets are transferred to a trust during their lifetime and then distributed to beneficiaries upon their death. Possessing a copy of the deceased veteran's living trust can provide critical information for estate planning and the distribution of assets, as well as help identify potential benefits for surviving family members.

Documents for Mortuary

DD214

WHEN MAKING FUNERAL arrangements, the mortuary will need to see a copy of the deceased veteran's DD214. This document provides essential information about their military service and confirms their eligibility for military honors at the funeral, such as the playing of Taps and the folding and presentation of the American flag.

Power of Attorney

THE MORTUARY MAY ALSO require a copy of the power of attorney, which grants a designated individual the authority to make decisions and act on behalf of the deceased veteran. This document ensures that the appropriate person is involved in making funeral arrangements and coordinating with the mortuary.

Marriage Certificate

IN SOME CASES, THE mortuary may request a copy of the marriage certificate to verify the relationship between the deceased veteran and their surviving spouse. This document can help establish the spouse's eligibility for certain benefits and provide necessary information for the funeral and burial arrangements.

Documents for Burial Benefit Form 21P-530

Death Certificate

WHEN SUBMITTING FORM 21P-530, the Application for Burial Benefits, a copy of the deceased veteran's death certificate is required. This document serves as official proof of the veteran's passing and is necessary to establish eligibility for burial benefits.

DD214

A COPY OF THE VETERAN'S DD214, or Certificate of Release or Discharge from Active Duty, must also be included with Form 21P-530. This document provides essential information about the veteran's military service, which is used to determine eligibility for VA burial benefits.

Copy of itemized funeral and burial bill showing expenses paid in full

A COPY OF THE ITEMIZED funeral and burial bill, showing that the expenses have been paid in full, must be submitted along with Form 21P-530. This documentation allows the VA to assess the costs incurred by the family and determine the appropriate amount of financial assistance to be provided.

Helpful Websites and Phone Numbers

Veteran Life Insurance (VGLI):

+1 800 669 8477

For information about life insurance policies for veterans, call the Veteran Life Insurance number to speak with a representative or visit their website.

Defense Finance and Accounting Service (DFAS):

+1 800 321 1080

For questions related to military pay, retirement benefits, and other financial matters, contact the Defense Finance and Accounting Service.

VA Regional:

+1 800 827 1000

To get in touch with your local VA regional office for assistance with benefits and services, call this number.

Social Security Office:

+1 800 772 1213

For information about Social Security benefits and services, including survivor benefits, contact the Social Security Office.

National Cemetery Scheduling Office:

+1 800 535 1116

To schedule a burial at a national cemetery, call the National Cemetery Scheduling Office.

VA Information:

[WWW.VA.GOV](http://www.va.gov)[1]

For comprehensive information about VA benefits and services, visit the VA's official website.

Military Records Request Online:

NARA | E-VETRECS TO request military records online, visit the National Archives and Records Administration's e-Vetrecs website. This platform allows veterans and their family members to request copies of essential military documents, such as the DD214.

---

1. http://www.va.gov

Chapter 7: Scams Veterans Must Avoid After Receiving Benefits

AS A VETERAN, YOU'VE selflessly devoted your time and energy to serving your country with honor and integrity. Now that you're entitled to receive benefits for your service, it's essential to remain vigilant against scams that specifically target veterans. Unfortunately, unscrupulous individuals may view your hard-earned benefits as an opportunity to exploit your trust and dedication. By being aware of the scams that target veterans and knowing how to protect yourself, you can ensure that you and your family can fully benefit from the assistance you've earned.

Scammers often employ a variety of deceptive tactics to lure veterans into their traps. They may use emotional appeals, high-pressure sales tactics, or even impersonate official government entities to gain your trust. It's crucial to recognize the warning signs and strategies that scammers use so you can avoid falling victim to their schemes. In the following sections, we'll delve into specific scams that target veterans, highlighting the tactics used by scammers and providing guidance on how to protect yourself and your benefits.

Types of Scams Targeting Veterans

Benefits Buyout Scam

Fraudulent offers to buy out benefits

ONE SCAM THAT TARGETS veterans is the Benefits Buyout Scam. In this scheme, scammers approach veterans with an enticing offer to buy out their future benefits in exchange for a lump sum of cash upfront. These offers may seem attractive, especially during times of financial hardship. However, these buyout proposals are often fraudulent and can lead to significant long-term financial losses for veterans.

Scammers involved in benefits buyout schemes typically offer an amount far less than the actual value of the veteran's benefits. Additionally, they may charge high fees and interest rates, leading to an even greater financial burden for the veteran. In some cases, veterans may unknowingly sign away their rights to future benefits, leaving them without the essential assistance they've earned through their service.

Dangers and potential consequences

THE DANGERS AND POTENTIAL consequences of falling victim to a Benefits Buyout Scam can be severe. By accepting an offer to buy out your benefits, you may be giving up a steady, reliable income that you and your family depend on. The lump sum you receive in exchange for your benefits may not last long, especially if you have ongoing financial needs or expenses.

Moreover, you may face legal complications if you unknowingly sign away your rights to future benefits. This could lead to difficulties in accessing essential services, healthcare, and support that you are entitled to as a veteran. Furthermore, the stress and financial strain caused by falling victim to a scam can have a negative impact on your mental and emotional well-being.

In order to avoid these dangers and protect your hard-earned benefits, it's crucial to be aware of the warning signs of a Benefits Buyout Scam and take steps to safeguard your financial future.

Charity Scam

Fake veteran charities

AS A VETERAN, YOU'VE demonstrated your unwavering commitment to your country, and it's only natural that you may want to support other veterans in need. However, it's essential to be cautious of fake veteran charities that prey on your compassionate nature. Scammers may create sham organizations that claim to support veterans and their families, but in reality, they pocket the donations for themselves.

These fraudulent charities often use emotional appeals and convincing stories to tug at your heartstrings. They may even adopt names and logos similar to those of legitimate organizations, making it challenging to distinguish between real and fake charities. To ensure that your hard-earned money goes to a genuine cause, take the time to verify the legitimacy of any charity before making a donation.

Crowdfunding fraud

WITH THE RISE OF ONLINE crowdfunding platforms, there has been an increase in crowdfunding fraud targeting veterans. Scammers may create fake fundraising campaigns, pretending to be a veteran in need or claiming to raise money for a veteran's medical bills, housing, or other essential needs. In reality, these deceitful individuals are only interested in lining their pockets with your donations.

As with fake charities, crowdfunding fraudsters often use emotional stories and images to convince potential donors of their sincerity. To protect yourself from falling victim to these scams, always research the individuals or organizations behind crowdfunding campaigns before donating. Look for evidence of their claims, such as in news articles, social media posts, or personal connections. By staying vigilant and informed, you can help ensure that your generosity benefits genuine veterans in need rather than falling into the hands of unscrupulous scammers.

Investment Scam/401(K) IRA

Fraudulent investment opportunities targeting retirement savings

AS A VETERAN, YOU'VE worked hard to build a secure financial future for yourself and your loved ones. However, scammers may try to exploit your hard-earned retirement savings by presenting fraudulent investment opportunities, specifically targeting 401(k) and IRA accounts. These deceitful schemes often promise high returns with minimal risk, playing on your desire to grow your nest egg and support your family.

Unfortunately, these too-good-to-be-true investment opportunities can result in significant financial losses, putting your retirement savings and future financial security at risk. In order to safeguard your hard-earned money, it's crucial to approach any investment opportunity with caution, carefully researching and verifying the legitimacy of the offer and the company behind it.

Warning signs of investment scams

RECOGNIZING THE WARNING signs of investment scams targeting veterans is vital to protecting your retirement savings. Some red flags to watch out for include:

- Unsolicited contact: Be cautious if you receive unsolicited phone calls, emails, or messages promoting investment opportunities, especially if they specifically mention your veteran status.
- High-pressure tactics: Scammers may try to pressure you into making quick decisions, claiming that their offer is time-sensitive or available only to a select few.
- Guaranteed returns: Be wary of investment opportunities that promise guaranteed returns or minimal risk; all investments carry some level of risk.
- Lack of transparency: Legitimate investment companies should be able to provide clear, detailed information about their investment products, fees, and risks.

Identity Theft Scam

Phishing emails and texts

IDENTITY THEFT IS A growing concern for everyone, including veterans. Scammers may use phishing emails and texts to steal your personal information, posing as government agencies, financial institutions, or other trusted organizations. These deceptive messages often request sensitive data, such as your Social Security number, bank account details, or login credentials, under the guise of updating your records or resolving an issue.

To protect yourself from identity theft, be cautious when receiving unsolicited emails or texts requesting personal information. Always verify the sender's authenticity before providing any sensitive data, and consider contacting the organization directly to confirm the request's legitimacy.

Social media impersonation

ANOTHER TACTIC SCAMMERS use to commit identity theft is social media impersonation. They may create fake profiles pretending to be veterans or veteran organizations, using these profiles to connect with you and gain your trust. Once they've established a connection, they may request personal information or attempt to lure you into scams.

To protect yourself from social media impersonation, be cautious when accepting friend requests or engaging with unfamiliar accounts, especially those claiming to be veterans or veteran organizations. Always verify the authenticity of these accounts before sharing personal information, and report any suspicious activity to the social media platform.

Trusted Resources for Veterans

Official government resources

Department of Veterans Affairs

THE DEPARTMENT OF VETERANS Affairs (VA) is a valuable resource for veterans seeking accurate and up-to-date information on their benefits and services. The VA can provide guidance on healthcare, education, vocational rehabilitation, home loans, and more. By utilizing the VA as a trusted resource, you can confidently access the support and assistance you deserve while minimizing the risk of falling victim to scams. Visit the VA's official website at www.va.gov[1] for more information.

---

1. http://www.va.gov/

Federal Trade Commission

THE FEDERAL TRADE COMMISSION (FTC) is a government agency committed to protecting consumers, including veterans, from fraudulent practices and scams. The FTC offers resources and tools to help you identify, avoid, and report scams. They also provide educational materials on various topics, such as identity theft, online security, and financial management. Visit the FTC's official website at www.ftc.gov[2] for more information and to access their resources.

Nonprofit organizations

Veterans service organizations

VETERANS SERVICE ORGANIZATIONS (VSOs) are nonprofit groups that support veterans and their families. These organizations often offer assistance with benefits claims, financial planning, employment services, and other essential resources. Some well-known VSOs include the American Legion, Veterans of Foreign Wars (VFW), and Disabled American Veterans (DAV). By partnering with a reputable VSO, you can access valuable support and resources while reducing the risk of scams targeting veterans.

Financial education and assistance programs

NUMEROUS NONPROFIT organizations and programs are dedicated to helping veterans improve their financial literacy and stability. These organizations often provide free or low-cost financial education, counseling, and assistance services. Some examples include the National Foundation for Credit Counseling (NFCC), which offers financial counseling for veterans, and the Consumer Financial Protection Bureau (CFPB), which has a dedicated Office of Servicemember Affairs that provides financial education and resources for veterans and their families. By utilizing these trusted programs, you can gain the knowledge and skills necessary to protect yourself and your family from financial scams targeting veterans. Your unwavering commitment to your country as a veteran is truly commendable. Now, it's essential to channel that same resilience

---

2. http://www.ftc.gov/

and tenacity to safeguard your hard-earned benefits and secure your financial well-being. Staying informed about the scams that target veterans and understanding how to spot them will help you prevent fraudsters from exploiting your trust and generosity.

Remember, being well-informed is your strongest defense. By educating yourself about the various scams and their tactics, you can effectively shield not only yourself but also your fellow veterans from the grasp of these deceitful individuals.

As a veteran, you have a community of support behind you. There are numerous reliable resources and organizations available to help you stay informed and protected against scams targeting veterans. Utilize these networks to ensure that you and your fellow veterans can fully benefit from the assistance and services you've earned through your service.

By staying vigilant, informed, and connected to the right resources, you can effectively safeguard your financial future and continue to honor the values you upheld during your time in service.

Chapter 8: Marriage

IT IS WITH GREAT EMPHASIS that I clarify that the intention of this chapter is not to target any specific gender or heighten existing concerns or paranoia around relationships. Rather, the objective is to shed light on the reality that some individuals, regardless of gender, may harbor ill intentions toward others, particularly veterans with valuable benefits. It is crucial to understand that this issue can impact anyone, and our focus should be cultivating awareness and fostering informed decision-making. Unfortunately, sometimes people see another person at their lowest and take advantage. Many veterans have been through a great deal, making sacrifices to serve their country, which leaves them a little drained and out of it. That's when most people who are looking to take advantage choose to make their move.

As I reflect on my own experiences, I am reminded of times when I witnessed situations that deeply impacted me. Seeing individuals being taken advantage of, particularly those who have selflessly served our country, is nothing short of heartbreaking. At times, I found myself feeling powerless to intervene, as some circumstances called for restraint and discretion. However, I believe these moments have given me the unique opportunity to share my insights and help others make well-informed choices.

It is through our collective experiences and the stories we share that we can build a supportive community, empowering veterans to make wise decisions that protect their hard-earned benefits and overall well-being. By discussing the potential pitfalls and challenges that may arise in relationships, we can provide guidance and encouragement to those who may be facing difficult choices.

In my own life, I have encountered situations where veterans were targeted by potential spouses who sought to exploit their benefits. This unsettling reality served as a stark reminder of the importance of making well-informed decisions, especially concerning matters of the heart. It is my hope that by sharing these experiences and shedding light on the potential risks, I can inspire others to approach their relationships with caution and discernment.

Through personal stories, shared experiences, and open dialogue, we can create a strong network of support for veterans navigating the complex world of relationships. It is my fervent belief that by doing so, we can help protect those who have sacrificed so much for our country, ensuring that their futures are filled with love, stability, and the respect they so rightfully deserve.

As we delve deeper into this chapter, it is crucial to keep in mind that the focus is on empowerment, awareness, and informed decision-making. The aim is not to induce fear or paranoia but rather to provide the necessary tools and insights for veterans to make well-informed choices about their relationships. It is through knowledge and understanding that we can cultivate a sense of empowerment, enabling veterans to protect themselves and their valuable benefits from those who may seek to exploit them.

One of the most valuable resources at a veteran's disposal is the collective wisdom and experience of fellow veterans. Connecting with others who have faced similar challenges and triumphs can provide a wealth of knowledge, guidance, and support. By engaging in conversations and sharing stories with one another, veterans can learn from the experiences of their peers and gain insights into the potential pitfalls and challenges they may encounter in their relationships.

Networking with other veterans can take various forms, from attending support groups and social events to participating in online forums and social media groups. These opportunities for connection can provide a safe space for veterans to share their thoughts, feelings, and experiences openly, fostering a sense of camaraderie and mutual understanding.

As veterans learn from one another's experiences, they can begin to identify patterns and potential red flags in their own relationships. By listening to the stories of others, they can gain a deeper understanding of the potential risks they may face and develop strategies to protect themselves and their hard-earned benefits.

Gathering Advice On How Not To Get Taken Advantage Of

BY LEARNING FROM THE experiences of others, networking with fellow veterans can provide invaluable advice and guidance on how to avoid or lessen the chances of being taken advantage of in relationships. By engaging in open dialogue and asking questions, veterans can gather practical tips and strategies to help safeguard their emotional and financial well-being.

Some advice that veterans may receive from their peers could include:

1. Taking time to truly know their partner: Building a strong foundation of trust and understanding in a relationship requires time and patience. Veterans should be encouraged to take the necessary time to truly know their partner, their values, and their intentions before making any long-term commitments.

2. Establishing clear boundaries: Setting clear boundaries regarding finances and personal matters can help protect veterans from potential exploitation. Openly discussing expectations and limits with their partner can foster a sense of mutual respect and understanding, making it less likely for misunderstandings or exploitation to occur.

3. Seeking professional guidance: In some cases, veterans may benefit from seeking the advice of professionals, such as financial advisors or legal counsel, to help safeguard their assets and benefits. These professionals can provide expert guidance on how to protect oneself from potential exploitation.

4. Creating a support network: Building a strong support network of friends, family members, and fellow veterans can provide a crucial safety

net for veterans navigating the complexities of relationships. This network can offer emotional support, practical advice, and a sounding board for discussing concerns or potential red flags.

5. Trusting their instincts: Finally, veterans should be encouraged to trust their instincts when it comes to their relationships. If something feels 'off' or concerning, it is essential to listen to that gut feeling and seek guidance or support as needed.

By networking with other veterans and gathering advice on how to avoid or lessen the chances of being taken advantage of, veterans can feel more confident and secure in their relationships. Armed with the knowledge, support, and guidance of their peers, they can make well-informed decisions that protect their emotional and financial well-being, ensuring a future filled with love, respect, and stability.

The Value of Veterans' Benefits

Explanation Of Various Benefits Earned Through Service

VETERANS' BENEFITS are a testament to the gratitude and respect our country holds for those who have selflessly served in the military. These benefits are earned through dedicated service and sacrifice, and they are designed to support veterans and their families as they transition back into civilian life. The benefits available to veterans cover a wide range of areas, reflecting the diverse needs of those who have served.

1. Healthcare: Veterans are eligible for healthcare benefits through the Department of Veterans Affairs (VA). These benefits may include access to medical centers, outpatient clinics, and other healthcare facilities that provide a range of services, such as preventative care, primary care, hospital care, and mental health services.
2. Education: The GI Bill and other education programs provide financial assistance to veterans pursuing higher education or vocational training. These programs can help cover the cost of tuition, fees, books, and

housing, enabling veterans to further their education and advance their careers.

3. Disability compensation: Veterans who have sustained injuries or developed medical conditions as a result of their military service may be eligible for disability compensation. This monthly benefit is intended to provide financial support to those who are unable to work or face other challenges due to their service-related disabilities.

4. Pension benefits: Some veterans may be eligible for pension benefits, which provide financial support to those with limited income and resources. These benefits are designed to help veterans maintain a basic standard of living and are based on factors such as age, disability, and financial need.

Home loan and housing assistance: The VA offers various programs designed to help veterans secure affordable housing, including home loan guarantees, grants for home adaptations, and rental assistance.

The Unfortunate Reality of Spouses Exploiting These Benefits

DESPITE THE NOBLE INTENTIONS behind veterans' benefits, there is an unfortunate reality that some potential spouses may see these benefits as an opportunity for exploitation. In some cases, individuals may enter into a relationship or marriage with a veteran with the primary goal of gaining access to their benefits rather than out of love or commitment.

This exploitation can manifest in various ways, such as by pressuring the veteran to apply for benefits they may not need, manipulating the system to maximize financial gain, or diverting the benefits for their own use rather than supporting the veteran and their family. In some extreme cases, spouses may even resort to deceit or fraud to gain access to these benefits, causing legal and financial complications for the veteran.

The emotional toll of such exploitation can be immense, as veterans may feel betrayed, used, or resentful toward their spouses. These feelings can exacerbate existing mental health challenges, such as PTSD, making it even more crucial for veterans to be aware of the potential risks and take steps to protect themselves and their benefits.

By understanding the value and importance of the benefits they have earned through their service, veterans can better recognize the potential risks associated with unscrupulous spouses. This awareness, combined with networking and support from fellow veterans, can empower them to make informed decisions about their relationships, ensuring that their hard-earned benefits are used for their intended purpose—to support and honor the sacrifices of those who have served our country.

Importance of understanding the risks and protecting benefits

AWARENESS OF THE POTENTIAL risks associated with relationships is essential for veterans who seek to protect their hard-earned benefits. By understanding the possible dangers, veterans can take proactive steps to safeguard their emotional and financial well-being, ensuring that their benefits are used to support themselves and their families as intended.

Some of the risks veterans may face in relationships include the following:

1. Financial exploitation: Unscrupulous spouses may attempt to gain control over a veteran's benefits, diverting them for their own use or pressuring the veteran to apply for unnecessary benefits.
2. Emotional manipulation: Some individuals may prey on a veteran's vulnerabilities, such as PTSD or feelings of isolation, to manipulate them into a relationship based on the potential financial gain from the veteran's benefits.
3. Legal complications: In some cases, spouses may resort to deceit or fraud to access a veteran's benefits, potentially resulting in legal battles and financial difficulties for the veteran.

To protect themselves from these risks, veterans must take a proactive approach to safeguard their benefits. Some protection measures can include:

1. Establishing financial boundaries: By setting clear financial boundaries with their partner, veterans can ensure that their benefits are used appropriately and not exploited for personal gain.
2. Seeking professional advice: Consulting with financial advisors, legal counsel, or other professionals can help veterans navigate the complexities of their benefits and protect themselves from potential exploitation.
3. Building a support network: A strong support network of friends, family, and fellow veterans can provide emotional support, practical advice, and a sounding board for discussing concerns or potential red flags in a relationship.

Being selective in choosing a spouse

ONE OF THE MOST EFFECTIVE ways for veterans to protect their benefits and emotional well-being is to be selective in choosing a spouse. This does not mean avoiding relationships altogether but rather approaching them with caution, discernment, and a strong sense of self-worth.

Some strategies for being selective in choosing a spouse include:

1. Taking time to truly know the person: This is pretty obvious as it is not only a life lesson for veterans but, in fact, for every human being. Know that developing a deep understanding of a potential partner's values, intentions, and character is essential before making any long-term commitments. By investing time and effort into building a strong foundation of trust and understanding, veterans can better assess the suitability of their partner and protect themselves from potential exploitation.
2. Observing behavior patterns: Paying close attention to a partner's behavior patterns can reveal important insights into their intentions. If a partner consistently demonstrates selfish or exploitative behaviors, this

may be a red flag that they are not genuinely committed to the veteran's well-being.

3. Trusting instincts: As said before, Veterans should trust their gut feelings when it comes to their relationships. Sometimes, your instincts can be the best guide for you to understand what is best for you and what is not.

4. Seeking external perspectives: Consulting with friends, family members, or fellow veterans can provide valuable insights and feedback on a potential partner. These external perspectives can help veterans assess the suitability of their partner and identify any potential concerns or red flags.

By being selective in choosing a spouse, veterans can increase the likelihood of building a healthy, supportive relationship based on love and respect rather than one rooted in exploitation or manipulation. This discerning approach, combined with a strong support network and an understanding of the potential risks, can empower veterans to protect their benefits, their emotional well-being, and their future.

Reasons to be selective

1. Pressure and manipulation to access benefits

ONE OF THE KEY REASONS for being selective when choosing a spouse is to protect yourself from individuals who may see your spousal benefits as a potential target. Some unscrupulous individuals may enter into a relationship or marriage with a veteran primarily to gain access to their benefits. They may exert pressure on the veteran to apply for these benefits, even when they are not necessary or manipulate the system to ensure they receive as much financial gain as possible. By being cautious and discerning in your choice of partner, you can minimize the risk of falling prey to such exploitation.

1. The impact of marrying someone interested only in benefits

Your choice of spouse has a profound impact on your future, both emotionally and financially. Marrying someone who is solely interested in your benefits can lead to a future of instability and uncertainty. You have worked very hard to earn your benefits, and you can't just hand them over to the first person that smiles at you. The exploitation of your benefits can result in financial strain and, in some cases, legal complications. Furthermore, a relationship based on ulterior motives often lacks the emotional support and genuine commitment necessary for a healthy, long-lasting partnership. Being selective in choosing a spouse helps ensure you are building a future with someone who values you for who you are rather than for the benefits you bring to the table.

1. Potential damage to mental health and well-being

Being in a relationship with someone who is only interested in your benefits can take a significant emotional toll. Veterans may already face challenges related to their military service, such as PTSD, and the additional stress of an exploitative relationship can exacerbate these issues. Feelings of betrayal, anger, and resentment can arise when a spouse prioritizes benefits over the well-being of the veteran, leading to long-lasting emotional harm. Being selective in choosing a spouse helps protect your mental health and overall well-being by ensuring you are in a relationship with someone who genuinely cares for you and supports you through life's challenges.

1. Awareness of risks and protective steps

In some cases, a spouse who is only interested in a veteran's benefits may resort to deceptive or fraudulent tactics to gain access to those benefits. This can involve filing false claims, manipulating the legal system, or even taking legal action against the veteran. It's crucial to be aware of these potential risks and take steps to protect yourself. Some protective measures include seeking legal advice, establishing clear financial boundaries, and building a support network of fellow veterans and trusted friends and family members.

Being selective in choosing a spouse is not about being distrustful or closed off to love; it's about ensuring that you are entering into a relationship based on genuine affection, respect, and commitment. By taking the time to get to know your partner, observing their behavior, and listening to your instincts, you can protect your benefits, your emotional well-being, and your future. You deserve a relationship that honors the sacrifices you have made in service to our country, and being selective in choosing a spouse is a crucial step toward achieving that goal.

The increased value of veterans after an honorable discharge

I ALWAYS TELL PEOPLE that an honorable discharge is just as valuable as any degree out there due to its potential when you fully utilize all the benefits you are entitled to. Degree holders, in many cases, still have to fill out job applications, while veterans utilizing their benefits properly upon receiving an honorable discharge can choose to work or live off of their recently obtained benefits. With that being said, I say a DD214 with the word 'Honorable' can be just as valuable or even more valuable than any degree. Sometimes a potential spouse can see your value before you do, and that's where you, the veteran, become vulnerable to the predatory behavior of others. It's good to keep the details of your benefits to yourself until you have really gotten to know new friends and potential spouses.

Upon receiving an honorable discharge, veterans often experience a significant increase in their value, both personally and financially. The benefits they have earned through their dedicated service to the country, such as healthcare, education, disability compensation, and pension benefits, not only serve to support them and their families but also make them an attractive target for individuals with ill intentions. This heightened value can, unfortunately, attract potential partners who may be more interested in exploiting these benefits than in forming a genuine, loving relationship.

In light of the potential risks associated with relationships, it is crucial for veterans to be selective when choosing a spouse. This does not mean avoiding relationships or being distrustful of all potential partners but rather approaching the search for a life partner with caution, discernment, and a strong sense of self-worth. By taking the time to truly know a person and carefully considering their intentions and character, veterans can protect themselves from entering into relationships that may result in the exploitation of their hard-earned benefits.

Being selective in choosing a spouse is also essential in ensuring that the chosen partner will provide the emotional support and genuine commitment necessary for a healthy, long-lasting relationship. A marriage based on mutual love, respect, and understanding not only provides a strong foundation for personal growth and happiness but also helps to safeguard the veteran's benefits and overall well-being.

As a veteran, it is essential to recognize your own worth and take active measures to protect your benefits. Acknowledging that your benefits are a valuable asset earned through your service to the country is the first step toward safeguarding them. Some strategies to protect your benefits and recognize your personal worth include:

1. Establishing financial boundaries: By setting clear financial boundaries with your partner, you can ensure that your benefits are used appropriately and not exploited for personal gain. This also helps to maintain a healthy balance of power and control in the relationship, preventing potential manipulation or abuse.

2. Building a support network: Connecting with fellow veterans, friends, and family members can provide you with valuable advice, emotional support, and external perspectives on potential partners. This support network can help you make informed decisions about your relationships and protect your benefits.

3. Trusting your instincts: It is important to listen to your gut feelings when it comes to your relationships. If something feels off or concerning, trust your instincts and seek guidance or support as needed.

This can help you identify potential red flags early on and take appropriate action to protect yourself and your benefits.

4. Seeking professional advice: Consulting with financial advisors, legal counsel, or other professionals can help you navigate the complexities of your benefits and protect yourself from potential exploitation. These experts can provide guidance on how to manage your benefits effectively and maintain control over your financial assets.

When you are selective in choosing a spouse, recognizing your personal worth, and taking proactive steps to protect your benefits, you must ensure that your hard-earned assets are used to support your well-being and that of your family. Ultimately, protecting your benefits is about honoring the sacrifices you have made in service to our country and ensuring that your future is built on a foundation of love, respect, and genuine commitment.

Chapter 9: Triple Dipping

———

ONE OF THE MOST VALUABLE yet often misunderstood concepts in the military is that of triple dipping. Triple dipping refers to the unique situation in which a veteran is eligible for and receives three types of benefits from the federal government simultaneously. Specifically, these benefits include retirement pay, VA disability compensation, and Social Security Disability. While this financial support can provide a much-needed safety net for retired veterans, it may also attract some criticism from those who might not fully understand the sacrifices you made to earn these benefits.

It's essential for the general public to recognize that veterans have devoted a significant portion of their lives to serving their country. The benefits they receive are not handouts but rather a reflection of the commitment and dedication they demonstrated throughout their military careers. However, there will always be individuals who do not see it that way. Some people might feel envious or even resentful of the support you receive, and they may criticize you for *taking advantage* of the system.

In order to maintain harmonious relationships and avoid unnecessary conflict, it's crucial to adopt a humble and discreet approach when discussing your benefits. Refrain from bragging about the financial support you receive and instead focus on the lessons you learned and the experiences you gained during your time in the military. By doing so, you can help mitigate any negative opinions others may have and foster an atmosphere of mutual respect and understanding.

In this chapter, we will dive deeper into the concept of triple dipping, explore the eligibility criteria, dig into the types of benefits involved, and learn how to file a claim with the VA. We'll also discuss the importance of seeking professional assistance to ensure you maximize the benefits you're entitled to receive. By the end, you should have a clearer understanding of this unique opportunity and be better equipped to make the most of the support available to you.

While it's important to be mindful of the feelings of others, never lose sight of the fact that you've earned these benefits through your hard work and dedication. By keeping this in mind, you can navigate the complex world of post-military life with confidence and the knowledge that you're making the most of the opportunities available to you.

With a strong foundation in place, you'll be better positioned to build a fulfilling and successful life after the military, one that honors the sacrifices you made and the values you upheld during your service. So, let's dive into the world of triple dipping and explore how you can make the most of these benefits to ensure a comfortable and secure future for you and your loved ones.

As you journey through this next chapter of your life, it's important to know the ins and outs of triple dipping eligibility. I know it can be overwhelming, but I'm here to help you break it down step by step. By understanding the criteria you need to meet, you'll be better prepared to secure the benefits you deserve.

First and foremost, to be eligible for triple dipping, you must have served a minimum of 20 years in the military. That's right, two whole decades of service. I'm sure you've got countless stories and experiences to share from that time, both good and bad. It's an incredible accomplishment, and you should be proud of reaching such a milestone. But the time spent serving your country doesn't just give you bragging rights—it also lays the foundation for your eligibility to receive these benefits.

Next, let's discuss the VA disability rating. To qualify for triple dipping, you must also have a disability rating from the VA. This rating reflects any service-related disabilities you may have and determines the amount of disability compensation you're entitled to receive. It's a difficult reality to face, but your time in the military may have left you with physical or mental health challenges that require ongoing care and support. This disability compensation is set aside by the military to help you manage these challenges and maintain the best quality of life possible.

Finally, there's the matter of limited income and assets. To be eligible for triple dipping, you must have limited income and assets. This means that your overall financial situation must fall within certain thresholds established by the federal government. While this criterion may seem restrictive, it's in place to ensure that the benefits are distributed to those who need them most.

So, there you have it—the three key eligibility criteria for triple dipping: 20 years of military service, having a VA disability rating, and limited income and assets. It's essential to familiarize yourself with these requirements and evaluate your unique situation to determine if you qualify.

I understand that facing these realities can be tough, but remember that you're not alone in this journey. Your fellow veterans, friends, and family are there to support you, and so am I. Together, we'll navigate this complex process and ensure that you have access to the resources and benefits you need.

As we move forward, it's important to stay positive and focused. While the road ahead may be challenging, it's also filled with opportunities to learn, grow, and build the life you've always wanted. Your time in the military has prepared you for this moment, and you have the strength, resilience, and determination to overcome any obstacles that may arise.

In the following sections, we'll delve into the types of benefits involved in triple dipping, learn how to file a claim with the VA and find out the importance of seeking professional assistance. By understanding these aspects, you'll be better equipped to make informed decisions and advocate for yourself and your future. It's time to explore the three types of benefits involved in triple dipping. We'll take a closer look at each one, discussing how they're earned, who they're designed to support, and how they can impact your life post-military. By understanding these benefits and the role they play in your financial security, you can take full advantage of them and create a solid foundation for your future. So, let's dive in and learn more about these benefits in a *how-to* style that'll make it easy for you to follow along.

Retirement Pay

Earned by serving a minimum of 20 years

AS WE MENTIONED EARLIER, one of the key requirements for triple dipping is serving a minimum of 20 years in the military. By reaching this milestone, you become eligible for retirement pay. This benefit is designed to provide a reliable source of income for the rest of your life.

Now, you may be wondering how the retirement pay is calculated. The calculation is based on your rank, years of service, and the year you entered the military. The Department of Defense uses a formula that takes these factors into account to determine your monthly retirement pay. To get started, visit the Defense Finance and Accounting Service (DFAS) website, where you'll find a retirement pay calculator that can help you estimate your monthly benefit.

Keep in mind that your retirement pay may be subject to taxes, so it's essential to plan accordingly. Consult with a financial advisor or tax professional to ensure you're prepared for any tax liabilities that may arise.

Disability Compensation

Awarded for service-related disabilities

ANOTHER SIGNIFICANT component of triple dipping is disability compensation. This benefit is awarded to veterans who have sustained service-related disabilities, whether physical or psychological. The VA assigns a disability rating based on the severity of your condition, which directly impacts the amount of compensation you receive.

To apply for disability compensation, you'll need to file a claim with the VA. Start by gathering all relevant documentation, such as medical records, service records, and any evidence that supports your claim. Once you have everything in order, you can submit your claim online through the VA's eBenefits portal or in person at a regional VA office.

The VA will then review your claim and determine your eligibility for benefits. This process can take several months, so be prepared to wait patiently. If your claim is approved, the VA will assign a disability rating, and you'll begin receiving compensation payments.

VA Pension

Need-based benefits for wartime veterans and their surviving spouses

FINALLY, WE COME TO the VA pension, a need-based benefit available to wartime veterans and their surviving spouses. This benefit is designed to provide financial support to those who have limited income and assets, helping them maintain a decent quality of life.

To be eligible for the VA pension, you must meet specific service requirements, such as having served at least 90 days of active duty, including at least one day during a period of war. Additionally, you must meet income and asset limitations set by the VA.

Applying for the VA pension involves a similar process as applying for disability compensation. Begin by gathering all necessary documentation, including proof of income, assets, and military service. Once you have everything in order, submit your claim online through the VA's eBenefits portal or in person at a regional VA office.

The VA will review your claim and determine your eligibility based on your financial situation, service record, and other factors. If you're approved, you'll begin receiving monthly pension payments to help cover your living expenses.

Understanding the types of benefits involved in triple dipping—retirement pay, disability compensation, and VA pension—is crucial to maximizing your financial security after leaving the military. Each benefit serves a unique purpose and provides essential support to help you maintain a comfortable and stable life post-service. By familiarizing yourself with these benefits and the processes involved in applying for them, you'll be better equipped to advocate for yourself and access the resources you need.

Moreover, don't underestimate the value of seeking professional assistance, whether it's from a financial advisor, a tax professional, or a veterans' benefits attorney. These experts can provide valuable guidance and support to ensure you're making the most of the benefits available to you.

Throughout this journey, always keep in mind that you've earned these benefits through your hard work, dedication, and sacrifices. Your service to your country is something to be proud of, and the benefits you receive are a testament to your unwavering commitment. Embrace the opportunities these benefits provide and use them as a springboard to build a fulfilling and successful life after the military.

Process of submitting a claim

Online or in-person

SUBMITTING A CLAIM with the VA can be done in two ways: online or in person at a regional VA office. The choice is yours, but let's take a moment to explore each option to help you decide which one is best for you.

Filing your claim online is a convenient and efficient method, allowing you to submit your claim from the comfort of your own home. The VA's eBenefits portal is user-friendly and provides clear instructions for submitting your claim. You'll need to create an account if you haven't already and log in to access the online application. In-person filing, on the other hand, can provide you with the opportunity to speak directly with a VA representative who can answer any questions you may have and offer guidance throughout the process. To file in person, locate your nearest regional VA office and schedule an appointment. Keep in mind that walk-in services may be limited, so it's best to call ahead and confirm availability.

Regardless of the method you choose, it's essential to gather all relevant documentation before submitting your claim. This includes medical records, service records, and any evidence that supports your claim for retirement pay, disability compensation, or VA pension benefits. Taking the time to organize your paperwork will not only streamline the application process but also increase the likelihood of a favorable outcome.

VA's review of the claim

ONCE YOU'VE SUBMITTED your claim, the VA will review it to determine your eligibility for benefits. This process can take several months, so it's important to be patient and prepared for a potentially lengthy wait. During this time, the VA may request additional information or documentation to support your claim, so be sure to respond promptly to any requests.

Determining eligibility for benefits

AFTER THOROUGHLY REVIEWING your claim, the VA will make a decision regarding your eligibility for benefits. If you're found to be eligible, the VA will notify you and provide information about your approved benefits, such as your disability rating and monthly compensation amounts.

If your claim is denied, don't be disheartened. The VA's decision is not always final, and you have the right to appeal. Keep in mind that appealing a decision can be a complex process, so it's crucial to seek professional assistance, such as a veterans' benefits attorney, to help guide you through the appeal process.

Receiving Triple Dipping Benefits

Simultaneous payment of retirement pay, disability compensation, and VA pension

CONGRATULATIONS! YOU'VE made it through the challenging process of filing your claim and have been deemed eligible for triple dipping benefits. This is a significant accomplishment. Now, it's time to discuss what this means for your financial future and how these benefits can provide much-needed support in your post-military life.

As a triple dipper, you'll receive simultaneous payments for retirement pay, disability compensation, and a VA pension. These three benefits, combined, can provide substantial financial assistance, easing the burden of medical bills, living expenses, and other costs related to your military service.

Each benefit serves a unique purpose and addresses specific needs, so it's crucial to understand how they work together to support your overall financial well-being. Retirement pay offers a reliable source of income based on your years of service and rank, ensuring you can maintain a comfortable lifestyle. Disability compensation addresses the financial impact of service-related disabilities, providing additional support based on the severity of your condition. Finally, the VA pension offers a safety net for wartime veterans and their surviving spouses who have limited income and assets, ensuring a basic quality of life.

Financial support for struggling veterans

IT'S ESSENTIAL TO RECOGNIZE that receiving triple dipping benefits is not a sign of greed or taking advantage of the system. Rather, it's a well-deserved support system for veterans who have given so much of themselves in service to their country. These benefits are designed to ease your transition to civilian life by offering financial stability and providing a foundation upon which to build a successful and fulfilling future.

As you begin receiving your triple dipping benefits, remember to use them wisely and responsibly. Create a budget that takes into account your monthly income and expenses, ensuring you're living within your means and planning for the future. Consider setting aside a portion of your benefits for savings, investments, or an emergency fund, providing additional security and peace of mind.

Seeking Professional Assistance

Importance of consulting a VA representative or experienced attorney

NAVIGATING THE WORLD of veterans' benefits can be complex and overwhelming, but you don't have to do it alone. Seeking professional assistance can make a significant difference in your ability to access the benefits you deserve and make the most of the opportunities available to you.

Consulting with a VA representative or an experienced veterans' benefits attorney can provide valuable guidance and support throughout the process. These professionals are well-versed in the intricacies of veterans benefits and can help you understand complex eligibility requirements, navigate the application process, and even represent you in appeals, should the need arise.

Complex eligibility requirements

AS WE'VE DISCUSSED throughout this journey, eligibility requirements for triple dipping can be complicated and challenging to navigate on your own. This is where professional assistance becomes invaluable, providing you with the expertise and support necessary to ensure you're meeting all the necessary criteria.

In addition to helping you understand eligibility requirements, a VA representative or attorney can also assist with gathering documentation, submitting your claim, and addressing any issues that may arise during the review process. By leaning on the knowledge and experience of these professionals, you'll be better equipped to navigate the complexities of the benefits system and secure the financial support you've earned.

Remember that receiving triple dipping benefits is a significant achievement that reflects your dedication and service to your country. These benefits provide crucial financial support, ensuring you can build a stable and fulfilling life after the military.

As you pursue these benefits, stay true to yourself, your values, and your goals. Embrace the opportunity to build a bright future for yourself and your loved ones, and never hesitate to seek support and guidance from your network and professional resources. Remember, you're not alone in this journey—there are countless veterans, friends, family members, and professionals who are eager to help you succeed.

Keep your head held high, your spirit strong, and your heart full of hope as you continue to forge your own unique path. Know that you have the skills, knowledge, and support you need to overcome any challenges and seize any opportunities that come your way. And above all, remember that you've earned the right to enjoy the benefits, freedom, and stability that come with the 20 years of service you've given to your country.

Chapter 10: Honoring our Veterans - Past, Present, and Future

---

THROUGHOUT HISTORY, men and women have stepped forward to defend their nations, their fellow citizens, and the values that bind them together. These brave souls, our veterans, have faced untold challenges and hardships, and many have made the ultimate sacrifices for their country. They have left behind families, friends, and the comforts of their homes to endure the harsh realities of war. As we pause to honor our past and present veterans, we must also take this opportunity to look to the future and ensure that their sacrifices are not forgotten.

The bonds that unite veterans are deep and enduring. They have shared the trials of combat forged in the crucible of war. They have carried the weight of the loss of friends and comrades who have fallen in battle. They have seen the best and worst of humanity, and they carry these experiences with them for the rest of their lives. It is our duty, as citizens and as fellow human beings, to acknowledge their sacrifices and express our deepest gratitude for their service.

Our veterans come from all walks of life, from every corner of our nation. They are our neighbors, our friends, and our family members. They are of every race, religion, and creed. They represent the best of our diverse nation and remind us that unity and shared purpose can overcome even the most daunting challenges. They have given us the gift of freedom, and it is our responsibility to honor their service by working together to build a better future.

The stories of our veterans are as varied as the number of individuals who have served. Some have faced the horrors of war, while others have supported their comrades from afar. All have contributed to the defense of our nation, and all deserve our gratitude. It is important to listen to their stories, to learn from their experiences, and to bear witness to their sacrifices. By sharing their stories, we honor their service and ensure that their memories live on.

As we honor our veterans, we must also consider the challenges they face upon returning home. The transition from military to civilian life can be difficult, and many veterans struggle with physical and emotional injuries sustained during their service. We must commit ourselves to providing the support and resources necessary to help our veterans heal and reintegrate into society. This includes access to quality healthcare, mental health services, education, and employment opportunities. By addressing these challenges, we not only honor our veterans but also invest in the future of our nation.

The legacy of our veterans extends far beyond the battlefields on which they fought. Their courage, dedication, and resilience serve as an inspiration to future generations. We must ensure that the values for which they fought—freedom, democracy, and justice—are upheld and protected. By teaching our children about the sacrifices of our veterans, we instill in them a sense of gratitude and responsibility, encouraging them to become active and engaged citizens.

Honoring our veterans also means recognizing and supporting the families who have stood by their side. The families of our veterans have made tremendous sacrifices, dealing with long separations, uncertainty, and the pain of loss. They have been the pillars of strength and support for our veterans, and their love and commitment deserve our admiration and respect. We must extend our gratitude not only to our veterans but also to their families, who have shouldered the burden of their loved ones' service.

Looking to the future, we must find ways to prevent the scourge of war and promote peace and understanding among nations. This is perhaps the greatest tribute we can pay to our veterans. We must work tirelessly to create a world in which the sacrifices they have made are no longer necessary. We must engage in diplomacy, foster dialogue, and seek common ground with those who may seem different from us. It is through these efforts that we can honor the legacy of our veterans and build a brighter future for all.

In an increasingly interconnected world, our collective security depends on our ability to understand and appreciate the experiences and perspectives of others. By promoting cultural exchange and fostering relationships between nations, we can work together to address the global challenges that threaten our shared prosperity. Our veterans have shown us the importance of cooperation, teamwork, and selflessness, and we must carry these lessons forward as we strive for a more just and peaceful world.

We must also ensure that future generations are prepared to defend our nation and our values, should the need arise. This means investing in our youth and providing them with the education, skills, and resources necessary to become the leaders of tomorrow. We must instill in them a sense of civic duty, a commitment to service, and respect for the sacrifices of those who have come before them. By nurturing their potential, we can create a future that is worthy of the sacrifices our veterans have made.

As we remember and honor our veterans, it is vital that we also recognize the importance of supporting organizations and initiatives that work to improve the lives of veterans and their families. These organizations play a crucial role in providing essential services and support to our veterans, helping them navigate the challenges they face, and ensuring that they receive the care and assistance they deserve. By supporting these organizations, we can show our appreciation for our veterans and contribute to their ongoing well-being and success.

Honoring our veterans—past, present, and future—is a responsibility that falls upon each and every one of us. It is a duty that transcends politics, race, and religion, for it is rooted in our shared humanity and our common love for freedom and justice. We must come together to express our gratitude, to support our veterans and their families, and to work toward a future that is free from the horrors of war. It is through our collective efforts that we can truly honor the sacrifices of our veterans and ensure that their legacy lives on, inspiring generations to come.

Let us always remember the price of freedom and the sacrifices made by our veterans. Let us honor them not just on Veterans Day but every day by striving to be the best citizens we can be and by working together to create a world that is more peaceful, more just, and more compassionate. In doing so, we will pay tribute to the men and women who have given so much to our nation and our future, and we will ensure that their sacrifices are never forgotten.

www.ingramcontent.com/pod-product-compliance
Lightning Source LLC
Chambersburg PA
CBHW050555160726
48003CB00002B/909